NEVER GOING HOME

BY BRIAN BARTON

FICTION
Brooklyn Girls Don't Cuddle

NONFICTION
Hans Is Dead
Words with Steve Jobs
You Watch for James

NEVER
GOING
HOME

T·F·C

NEW YORK

CONTENTS

SIT BACK, RELAX, AND ENJOY

SHINY SIDE UP

PLEASE BE SEATED

For J.Y.

1

"YOU'D DEFINITELY KNOW THEIR NAME, but they wouldn't have had the same success. U2's career was made that one day in London, and it's all because Bono saved the girl," Matt says.

"What do you mean, 'Bono saved the girl?'"

"You know, he saved her," Matt says.

"Saved her *how*? Physically? Spiritually?" I ask. The JFK ground crew is wrapping up and the tug driver has attached the claw to the nose wheel. "You know what? Forget it."

"Why are your panties in a bunch, sir?"

"You know why."

"No, I don't, sir. *Why?*"

"No more monologues. Not now, Matt. Please," I say.

"Sir, seventy thousand people showed up on that one day in London—that's enough people to fill 140 triple-sevens. Live Aid was the most ambitious musical event in history and it was broadcast to over two billion people around the globe."

"Matt, contact the ramp for pushback."

"Let me paint the picture. It's a warm July afternoon and the crowd has been baking in the sun all day. And, sir, these people want to rock."

"Ramp control," I say.

"Right away, sir. So this four-piece combo takes the stage a little before 5:00 P.M. The front man is this scrawny little thing in a bolero jacket, and a mullet lies taxidermied on his head. Frankly, sir, Bono looks like a bellboy from Hotel Nowhere. But you have to understand the moment, sir. It's Wembley Stadium, the Carnegie Hall of rock and roll."

"We're not doing this. Not today. They closed the cargo door and we're ready to push. Parking brake released at 17:22 to mark departure. Call the ramp for clearance," I say.

"Right away, sir. So Bono steps up to the mic and says, 'We're an Irish band. We come from Dublin City, Ireland. Like all cities, it has its good. It has its bad. This is a song called '*Bad*.'"

I scowl, so Matt clicks his mic and sighs, then runs a hand through his hair and switches to COMM 1.

"Ground control, RASH three-five-eight, ready to push gate one-five," Matt says. The radio squawks with static and ground control is in our ears.

"*RASH three-five-eight, clear to push gate one-five.*"

"Clear gate one-five. RASH three-five-eight," Matt says, and looks at me. "Happy?"

"Overjoyed."

"U2 launch into '*Bad*' and it's like this invisible force surges into the band from the crowd. The audience is showing their love for the lads and the band is buoyed by the spirit. Sir, the hearts of the audience are now beating outside their bodies and it's a palpable feeling that wasn't there even a moment before. Musical history is about to be written, but nobody knows it. Not the crowd and definitely not the band."

"But this was one of U2's early shows," I say.

"Nothing will ever be the same in rock and roll after this night—and it's all because Bono saved the girl."

Matt navigates through a stack on his screen as his hair bristles in the air vent overhead. Sunlight streams through the cockpit windows, illuminating him in silhouette like a rock star on stage.

"Reach out to the tug on the comms to coordinate the push," I say.

"The Edge's Stratocaster has only one sound, sir: truth. His soundscape echoes through the stadium like a melodic call to arms. Meanwhile, Larry and Adam are tight in the backbeat driving the locomotion with Adam on stage left. Each cymbal crash is like an exclamation point on the melody while the bass lines stir the soul."

"We want an on-time departure, Matt." I shoot him another look.

"This will only take another minute, sir. You've never seen an audience so electrified." He returns to his cockpit screen but seems lost in thought. "And that's when Bono saves the girl."

"Stop saying that! What do you mean, 'Bono saves the girl?'" I say.

"Everything starts off OK. Bono's belting out the lyrics as a few Irish flags and banners stir the sky down in front. But halfway through the song, he drops the mic and bolts from the stage like a prison escapee. He jumps down to the press

13

platform below—the crowd *erupts*. He's waving his arms in the air like a man on a sinking ship. Maybe he's waving to some girls to come and join him, right? Meanwhile, these security dudes in yellow windbreakers are trying to defend the stage from the crush of the crowd."

"Frankly, sir, stadium security is clueless and they don't know what the fuck Bono's doing. Their job is to make sure seventy thousand screaming fans don't overrun the stage, but then they figure it out. He wants them to pull a girl standing a few hundred feet away out of the crowd. Security does their best to reach her, but it's like that arcade game with the claw and the plastic cube full of toys. You use the claw like a pair of forceps to extract the best toy, but you never get what you want."

"Anyway, security can't reach the girl and Bono isn't having it. Meanwhile, the band plays on in hopes their lead singer will return. That's when he moves to the edge of the stage and dangles off the side. He drops down to crowd level and the stadium erupts. I'm talking *bananas*, sir. Dozens of press and security rush him. Now he's deep in the mêlée. What the fuck, right? Meanwhile, his antics are being shown live to everyone at the stadium on a giant video screen, as well as being broadcast to billions of people around the globe," Matt says.

"Shit."

"Right? So security finally get to the girl and they hoist her over the barricade. Her legs and arms are in the air, she lands on the performers' side of the barrier, and rushes into Bono's arms. The two of them slow dance to '*Bad*' and the crowd loses its shit. I'm talking *double bananas*," Matt says.

"But—"

"Watching the footage of U2 at Live Aid leaves you with questions, am I right, sir? Was this some theatrical rock star trick to make the band look cool? To make a girl feel special? The cynic in you calls it tasteless showmanship because a cute girl is picked from the crowd and gets a special dance. Now everyone thinks you're the rock star with the heart of gold. You see where I'm going with this?"

"Yeah, but–"

"But after the show, the truth comes out. The girl wasn't chosen for a dance. She was rescued because she was being crushed to death—she couldn't breathe. Bono saw her struggling and got security involved. He saved her life."

"Matt, I–"

"Think of the artists that played that day in London, sir. Sting. David Bowie. Elton John. Phil Collins. Paul McCartney. The Who. Queen with Freddie Mercury. Freddie *fucking* Mercury, sir. But all anyone remembers is U2." Matt pauses and fidgets with the college ring on his finger.

"So, what happened to the girl, Matt?"

"What girl?" he says.

"The girl Bono saw! The one security rescued so she wasn't crushed. Thank god they got to her. What happened to her?"

"Sir, Live Aid is U2's launch pad. The band goes on to record fourteen platinum albums. *Fourteen.* They sell more than 170 million records in a career spanning more than four decades. Their income surpasses The Rolling Stones, Metallica, Paul McCartney, and Aerosmith. In 2001, U2 perform the most watched Super Bowl half-time show in history. Later, the band lands on the cover of *Time* and Bruce Springsteen inducts them into the Rock and Roll Hall of Fame. They go on to win twenty-two Grammy awards. *Twenty-two.* That's more Grammys than the

Beatles or Elvis or Madonna or Michael Jackson. More Grammys than any musical group on earth. Sir, U2 go on to become the most successful rock band in history."

"I get that, but what happened to *her*?" I ask.

"Who?" Matt says.

"The girl! The girl Bono saved! What happened to her?!"

Matt shrugs. "Does it matter?"

• • •

You want a girl because you want to be overwhelmed by the feminine: long hair spilling on your pillow, soft lips on yours, hips in your hands, arms holding you close. A naked girl means warmth, and warmth means love. Besides, summertimes are made for flings, and nakedness feels good.

Seeing a dress or skirt lying crumpled on your bedroom floor sends you because these are trophies from the hunt and proof of the kill. They're the small rewards of manhood you get in exchange for your sacrifices in the club of men.

Intimacy is like payment for your higher rates of cancer, alcoholism, suicide, diabetes, heart disease, and early death. It's what you get in exchange for inhaling thousands of pounds of jet exhaust during a decades-long career.

And if you're lucky, sex is the ultimate reward—it's compensation for your insomnia, personal demons, and private pain. It's a small token of thanks, a participation trophy from a middle-school basketball league.

"We clear to push?" you say.

"Yes, sir. *It's on.*"

"Run the before-start checklist, buddy boy."

"Roger that, sir. Running before-start checklist."

You're blind, so they push you into the alley and you pray, but you're on edge, skittish, with only one thought on your mind: Don't hit anything. It can happen—a push can go bad—and your biggest fear is fire. Running over a fuel truck as the tug pushes the 385 thousand-pound jet out of the gate would end badly. The resulting explosion would instantly incinerate you, your crew, and the two hundred fifty-eight passengers on board, sending a fireball thousands of feet into the sky and engulfing the surrounding jets at the gate. The conflagration would belch a plume of black smoke so thick it could be seen as far away as Hoboken, and the remains of your airframe would land in a crater fifty feet deep and a thousand feet across.

"Cleared to start one and two," says the tug over your headset.

The tug driver who pushes the jet from the gate must give the all clear to start the engines because ground personnel work in close proximity to the giant turbines. A worker could get sucked into the front of a six thousand pound engine or get roasted by the exhaust out the back—and neither option is desirable.

"Clear to start one and two," you reply to the tug, then look at your first officer. "Turn number one." Matt powers up the left engine. There's a rumble as it spins up and a whine fills the cockpit.

"One is online."

"Turn number two, buddy boy."

Your first officer is in full battle mode now, working with ground control and reviewing the flight plan and checklists. The turbines play for you in stereo like a high-pitched serenade. The plane rolls backward.

You're ashamed to admit your fondness for Matt—HazMatt, you call him—has turned parental, probably due to the age difference. You're the major leaguer and he's the promising upstart fresh from the farm leagues, both of you sitting side by side like a husband and wife on a car trip.

"RASH three-five-eight, contact tower on one-two-zero-point-niner for taxi. Goodnight."

"RASH three-five-eight, tower for taxi. Goodnight," Matt says to ground control. Your first officer's verbatim radio repetition is protocol, a verification standard designed to reduce errors. Matt's face is illuminated by the cockpit screens as he changes channels and broadcasts again. "Tower, RASH three-five-eight, request taxi clearance."

"Is the taxi checklist complete?" you say.

"Still working, sir."

"I want an on-time arrival, HazMatt. Let's move."

The view from where you sit would be the envy of any king or head of state. Emeralds of the Irish countryside have welcomed you during Dublin approach. The Aurora borealis has enchanted you over Anchorage night skies. Even the descent into Heathrow with the Tower Bridge, the Thames, the Eye, and Big Ben has given you sustenance like a full English breakfast. But your favorite view has to be the Alps, with those jagged brown peaks that jut up from the earth like almonds in a pint of rocky road. These sights prove what you've always known: The cockpit is the last, best front-row seat.

But your love affair with the skies started much earlier and the Blue Angels, the U.S. Navy's precision flying team, were your first crush. Their acrobatics had you mesmerized and you drooled at their gleaming F/A-18s because they were screamingly fast and deafeningly loud with remarkable agility in the air. Barreling through blue skies, the F/A-18 was as poetic as it was dangerous, like an arrow in flight.

As a child, watching the Blue Angels at Jones Beach over Memorial Day was one of your favorite summertime treats, and it still is as an adult. It's one of your favorite summertime activities—one of them, but not the only one—because you've acquired another taste: pulchritudinous young things.

Junior Captain. Your job title sounds like a Fisher-Price toy for four-year-olds. But it's not your title that bothers you—it's your place in the pilot hierarchy. You've ascended the ranks beyond first officer but haven't made it to senior captain, stuck in a kind of aviation purgatory waiting for one of those coveted spots to open up.

RASH Airlines has a seniority system, after all, which means the senior captains get the best of everything and you make do. You accept the routes the senior captains are loathe to travel, and that's been the secret to your success at RASH Airlines: being agreeable. Now everyone sees you as the go-to guy, the problem solver. *Go see Clay*, they say. *He'll help.*

Except you're fried and out of gas from the layovers and the "turns." Sure, a Boston or island turn (round trip) from New York City and back on a sunny day is fine. A Beantown or Bahamas turn under blue skies is a delight to be savored and enjoyed.

But double turns, two round trips in the same day, are more common, and as much fun for a pilot as an engine fire. These trips require more prep and ground work, and are more cognitively demanding. Flying time is what pilots crave and is where the good money is. But the senior captains take the good turns and leave the scraps to junior captains like you.

You lift the handset from the cradle and a chime rings out to remind you the P.A. is on.

FOLKS, GOOD EVENING FROM THE FLIGHT DECK. THIS IS CAPTAIN SONNERING AND WITH ME IN THE COCKPIT IS FIRST OFFICER BLANCANDO. ON BEHALF OF THE ENTIRE CREW, I'D LIKE TO WELCOME YOU ABOARD RASH AIRLINES FLIGHT #358 WITH SERVICE INTO HEATHROW IN LONDON, ENGLAND. OUR FLYING TIME FROM NEW YORK WILL BE JUST OVER SEVEN HOURS. WE HAVE A CHARMING CABIN CREW TO TAKE CARE OF YOU THIS EVENING. IF THERE'S ANYTHING WE CAN DO TO MAKE YOUR FLIGHT MORE COMFORTABLE, DON'T HESITATE TO ASK. WE INVITE YOU TO SIT BACK, RELAX, AND ENJOY YOUR JOURNEY WITH US. THANK YOU FOR CHOOSING RASH.

• • •

The push is successful and the tug removes the claw from the front gear, bathing the ramp in amber from its rooftop strobe. I grab the tiller, turn the nose wheel toward the taxiways, and give her some thrust. COMM 1 is busy with Friday evening radio traffic and ATC (air traffic control) is reaching out to multiple call signs.

"How we doing on the checklist, HazMatt?"

"It's complete, sir."

"Contact tower on 120.9 for taxi clearance."

"I did, sir. No word."

"Try again."

"RASH three-five-eight. Taxi to bravo, juliet, and cross one-three left at delta and remain on this frequency."

"And there it is," Matt says with a smile as he squeezes the trigger on his side stick. "RASH three-five-eight, bravo, juliet, and cross one-three left at delta."

Planes on the taxiways are lined up nose to tail like elephants at a circus. Matt whistles, "Now there's a jumbo jumble."

"Sterile cockpit. No talking until ten thousand feet," I say.

The manifest tells our story: two-hundred fifty-eight passengers and nine crew, Heathrow bound from JFK. All of us entombed in a $125 million dollar pressurized cigar tube filled with 110 thousand pounds of flammable jet fuel.

"Sir, what happened to adventure? To experience? You don't arrive at the Pyramids of Giza on camel back. You arrive via air-conditioned minibus, then snap a selfie in front of the Sphinx. That's not an experience," Matt says.

"After ten thousand feet, HazMatt. Your story can wait."

"Human experience requires struggle, sir. It demands it. You have to push up against something in order to grow. Wisdom isn't trips to India, consulting with yogis, or horseshit self-actualization. Only adversity creates self-mastery."

"You know how I feel about your monologues. Sterile cockpit." I bump the throttle and move us toward the taxiway markings for *bravo*.

"Only veterans and old people are wise, sir, because they've been through some fucked-up shit."

"Sterile cock—"

"But we don't listen to them, sir. We shove them in jails and nursing homes after their hard-earned wisdom...Be honest with me, sir. When was the last time you were pushed? Pushed to the limit. Really, sir. *When?*"

"The video cameras tell all," I say, turning the tiller to move us onto *juliet*.

"Video cameras, sir?"

"There and there," I say, pointing to two tiny cameras suction-cupped to the windshield with their lenses on us.

"The little silver camera you stuck on the glass?"

"Cameras, *plural*, HazMatt. One recording your side and one recording mine."

"I gotta be honest with you, sir. It's like you've got a surveillance fetish."

"I'm going to edit the video into something cool, maybe give it a *Top Gun* soundtrack."

"Very eighties, sir."

"The cameras stick to anything and record video for up to a month. I stuck some outside our offices at the terminal."

"They're kind of disco, sir," Matt says yanking on one of the glittery silver boxes.

"Don't touch! I spent twenty minutes setting them up and I need to take them off after we land."

"Sir?"

"*What!?*"

"Your hobby is weird."

"Noted, HazMatt."

"Travel is nothing but oxycodone for the soul, sir. A vacation is the only way the salary man can deal with another year at the job he can't stand, so he books a trip and suffers in some sort of cosmic bargain with the universe: 'If I suffer at my job, I'll be rewarded by a magical journey.' The salary man imagines a vacation filled with sex, white-sand beaches, limestone cliffs, and forever friendships. But his trip never delivers and he returns home sunburned, out of cash, and even sadder than when he left. And his memory is filled with the melancholy of foreign whores."

"And here I thought you were hiking in Bangkok."

Matt laughs. "Come on. You know you agree. Travel is nothing more than salt, fat, sugar, and carbs washed down with diet soda. We're the problem, sir. It's us. Air travel."

I follow the taxiway markings and come to a stop at the runway intersection where our taxiway, *delta*, meets one of the active runways.

"Recheck with tower we have permission to cross one-three left."

"Yessir," Matt says, opening his mic. "Tower, RASH three-five-eight, request permission to cross one-three left at delta."

"RASH three-five-eight, cleared to cross one-three left at delta and hold runway two-two right."

"Cross one-three left delta and hold two-two right, RASH three-five-eight," Matt says.

It's one of the things they teach you in ground school: Never cross an active runway without a visual check. You verbalize and verify the old-fashioned way to ensure you're not greeted by a triple-seven roaring down the runway at 170 knots at the end of his roll.

"Clear on the left," I say looking out my window like a child at a crosswalk.

"Clear on the right," Matt says.

"Continue and hold short of two-two right," I say giving her more thrust.

"I know, sir. Hold at two-two right."

"Contact tower again, HazMatt."

"What's the hurry? Give me a second, sir."

"We're burning fuel and time."

"Be chill, kimo," he says, opening his mic: "Tower, RASH three-five-eight, ready for departure on two-two right." He turns to me. "Happy?"

"Overjoyed."

"You don't have to be a dick, Mr. Company Man." A hiss fills the cockpit as Matt adjusts the air nozzle over his head, smacking his lips. "We're number two after the seven-six at two o'clock. Watch out for his wake." He rummages in his flight bag and upends the contents on the cockpit floor. "Coulda sworn I had water. *Fuck me.*"

"Calm down, man. Here." I hand him one of my water bottles and he hoists it in thanks like I bought him a beer, downing the contents and dribbling some on his shirt. The plastic bottle crinkles in his fist and the noise fills the cockpit.

"That's going to get annoying."

"What's going to get annoying?" Matt says.

"You know what."

"No, I don't, sir. *What?*"

"The crinkling. *You.* Please stop."

"You're so sound-sensitive." Matt squeezes the bottle again like a baby with a toy and cracks himself up. He holds the bottle up to my ear and gives it a few more pumps, then peals with laughter.

"Mature. Real mature."

"Couldn't resist, sir. It gives me such pleasure...Name the place for the climb out. Fukoka. Bitburg. Domodedovo. Sheremetyevo. Everyone speaks English on the comms because we're the fucking lingua franca of the skies." He looks at his watch and syncs it against the flight computer. "Imagine if we weren't back-to-back World War champs."

I sigh loudly.

"Straight up, sir. That's why I like flying with you. Let's flip for the takeoff roll."

This month marks my two-decade anniversary with RASH Airlines and means I've finally got some options. It's an important milestone in any junior captain's career because it means you can apply for senior captain and rise in the ranks. For me, it means I can finally build a balanced life in New York along with the career upgrade.

Sure, there's a fatter paycheck and more prestige at the senior captain level, but that's not what I'm after. What I want is first shot at the best turns and layovers so I can have a steady schedule. I can start working out again, take some classes, get a handle on my debt, and maybe fix up my apartment.

Matt sets the brake, I grab the thrust control levers and push them forward. The plane groans against the conflicting inputs as we lay in wait like a sprinter at the starting blocks. Ninety thousand pounds of thrust in my hands and the plane's begging me for flight—and I can't wait to oblige.

Our engines are like enormous vacuum cleaners, sucking in air and belching out thrust and exhaust. Plus, they're the only truth-in-advertising left because they actually deliver on their hyperbole: *Power! Adventure! Thrills!*

A jet engine up close reveals geometries of conical and angular forms that invite lust and caution. The gigantic housing, fan blades, exhaust ducts, and intakes are engineered to a millimeter's precision, then machined to perfection. An engine is as smooth as glass and tough as a tank, but she's no princess for a day—she demands to be heard like the thunder of a shinkansen roaring through the dawn.

There's a squawk of static over our headsets like an old man clearing his phlegm: *"RASH three-five-eight, cleared for takeoff runway two-two right. Wind two-seven-five at five knots. Fly heading zero-seven-zero."*

"RASH three-five-eight, roger. Cleared for takeoff on two-two right, heading zero-seven-zero," Matt says.

The plane's exterior lights are on and our blinking wing tips can be seen for miles in any direction. Our landing lights illuminate the runway in front of us as I pick up the P.A.

> THIS IS THE CAPTAIN AGAIN. FOLKS, WE'VE BEEN CLEARED FOR TAKEOFF AND WILL BE DEPARTING MOMENTARILY. FLIGHT ATTENDANTS, PLEASE BE SEATED.

• • •

You push the thrust levers forward and lurch into the darkness with a roar at your back. You're moving faster, picking up speed, until a bump jostles you from your seat and the flight harness squishes you back down like a hand. You give the side stick a little bit of forward pressure as you roll, but you're longing inside because you're still on terra firma.

You're accelerating down the runway with feet on the rudder pedals, steering like a soapbox derby racer with eyes "outside" on the runway as you build speed. Meanwhile, Matt's eyes are "inside" and on the instruments so he can make callouts based on his readings.

"Forty knots airspeed alive...sixty knots...eighty...thrust set," he says.

"Light and sweet."

"*Eee-per* is good. N1, N2, EGT within range...ninety," Matt says.

"*Blue skies smilin' at me. Nothin' but blue skies do I see.*"

You continue with the forward pressure on the stick as your momentum builds, then relax your grip to neutral as you reach one hundred knots. Earth and sky tempt you in this viscous limbo.

"One-twenty," Matt says.

Departures flit past your window like fence posts on a highway and you double-check the airspeeds to ensure the needles are indeed off the pegs. But safety is always top of mind, and your right hand rests on the thrust levers in case you need to abort.

"One-forty...one-sixty...V1," Matt says.

V1 is decision speed, which means a judgment call must be made: takeoff or abort. But there are no engine problems or critical issues to attend to, so you commit to flight by removing your hand from the thrust levers. V1 passes and it's just as well because you can't abort the takeoff if you wanted to—there isn't enough runway left to stop.

Now you're in a suburban kitchen crying because the peanut butter sandwich in front of you isn't sliced in the rectangles you prefer. You complain in the only way you know how until a yellow telephone wallops you in the head. The base crunches against your skull and your head bounces off the table. You're in hysterics, crying with snot pouring from your nose, and the phone connects with your skull again. And now you're back.

"Rotate."

Your first officer's directive means it's time to pull back on the stick so you'll rise skyward. All you need to do is give the stick a little bit of a tug and you'll take off...or...or you could rocket down the runway until you run out of space. Sure, you've thought about it, but kept those dark urges to yourself, even if something occasionally did slip out.

Maybe you'd be out for drinks with some of the guys or talking shit with someone in the ready area and you'd say something dark to lighten the mood. A macabre phrase might tumble through your lips like some errant spittle.

Except you were no wackadoo, no weirdo or psycho. Sure, you had your issues—everyone did—but you were healthier than most by a long shot. You just acknowledged these dark urges and that was OK in your book. Everyone's thought of suicide, but you'd never once had the desire at the controls.

Never.

But last summer in Connecticut, some thoughts had surfaced. You let your mind wander while driving alone at night on a two-lane highway. You were doing 90 mph in a 65 zone, rock music blaring, singing at the wheel—not a care in the world. Except you had the tiniest tickle of a feeling, like a tear was stuck in the corner of your eye.

A car crested a rise in the distance and its headlights shone like a beacon in the darkness. You watched it racing toward you and thought of a way you might change the path you were on. Maybe you could erase all that was and would be. *What if you could start again?*

You flicked a few buttons on the stereo and looked up to find the car closing fast with only a double-yellow line separating you. *What if things were different?* And then it came to you—an idea—so you steeled yourself as the car sped toward you.

One hundred and fifty yards away, one hundred. *Ready?* You pressed down hard on the accelerator and gripped the wheel tightly. *Set?* You clenched your jaw and held your breath. Fifty yards away. Twenty-five yards. *Go?*

All it would take is one flick of the wrist—less effort than it would take to wave goodbye—to change everything. You'd nudge the car a little to the left and cross the yellow line and *poof*, no more dirty dishes in the sink. No more birthdays alone.

Except you weren't a sick fuck and you could have your sad thoughts while still being in control yourself, because that was the power of being a man. And you weren't the type to kill an innocent driver or everyone onboard a plane because you were having a shitty day, month, year, or whatever. No way.

A hand is shaking your shoulder and there's a loud noise in your ear. It's a voice that's shouting your name.

"Clay! Rotate! Pull up!" Matt shouts.

Your eyes open to find the side stick in a death grip like a choke hold and the jet rollicking along the emergency runway extension. You close your eyes and try to wish the scene away.

PRIORITY RIGHT.

The flight computer's aural notification tells you the stick in your hand has been de-prioritized and your flight controls are gone. Control for the aircraft is now with your first officer and Matt grabs his stick, pulling hard, struggling to bring the jet off the ground.

"She's mine!" he shouts.

"I'm sorry. I—"

29

"Stand down. My airplane."

He pulls on the stick and the jet's nose rises sharply off the runway until the engine noise transforms into a soothing dull hum and the horizon disappears.

"I got–" he says.

Your body is in free fall until a sharp pain like a punch slams into the back of your head. The flight harness digs into your skin and your neck snaps back against the headrest. A jolt rocks the cockpit.

"Fuck!" Matt shouts. The plane shudders, then lists side to side like a leaf in the wind.

SPEED. SPEED. DON'T SINK, says the flight computer.

You look out the window at the glowing runway, its parallel lines like a scar on the belly of the landscape. Your eyes close and your head slumps to your chest.

"Sir! Declare an emergency, begin checklist, and notify crew," Matt says.

The words register faint like a faraway radio call as a thick fog envelops you. You try to speak but can't move your lips.

"JFK tower, RASH three-five-eight, declaring an emergency. Request radar vector for immediate landing," Matt says. The flight computer is barking orders like a drill sergeant and COMM 1 squawks with static.

UNDERSPEED. BANK ANGLE, says the flight computer.

"JFK tower, RASH three-five-eight, declaring an emerg–" Matt says.

SPEED. DON'T SINK.

An unintelligible radio voice responds in a flurry of static.

"Repeat. JFK tower. Repeat," Matt says.

"RASH three-five-eight, JFK tower. Clear to land two-one right."

"RASH three-five-eight, clear on two-one right," he says.

Your eyes blink open and you reach for the side stick and find it dull and unresponsive.

UNDERSPEED. <SIREN> <SIREN>

"They're..."

"What?!" Matt says. "*What?!*"

TERRAIN. TERRAIN. PULL UP. PULL UP.

"They're on the move. They're coming."

"Sir? *Sir!?* Oh god. *Sir!*"

2

KATRINA SLAMMED THE CAR DOOR and looked up at the sky as engine sounds crackled the air and a jet roared overhead. The plane banked right over JFK with turbofans at maximum thrust and then climbed higher, leaving a brown plume in its wake.

There was a noise coming from inside the car and Katrina turned to peer through the open passenger window. Sumito was staring at her with gloved hands on the wheel.

"The terms of your contract are clear," he said.

"Per Hillingdon," Katrina said.

"Be at the RV on time. We won't be waiting for you."

"Understood."

"And don't cock up, love," said a woman's voice from the back seat. Petrova, a petite brunette with a big nose, took out a high-tech walkie-talkie and spoke into her headset. "Comms check, one-two," she said, and Katrina's earpiece squealed with static.

"Bloody hell!" Katrina pulled out her earpiece. "Turn that fucking thing down!" She stared daggers at Petrova through the window.

"We're five by five," Petrova said with a smile, then adjusted the gain on the equipment.

"Don't be a wanker, Pet. Your encrypted radios are dodgy at best."

"AES-256 is the tits, love. We've got power and range and can stomp on comms from air traffic and law enforcement. My system is bombproof. Now, off you go. I even packed you a lunch." She sneezed.

"Bless you," Sumito said, handing Petrova a handkerchief.

"Sod off, Pet. Watch a grown up at work." Katrina inserted the wireless transmitter back into her ear and turned away.

"The RV, Katrina," Sumito said through the open car window. "Be there. On time."

"Toodles, love!" Petrova said.

"Cunt."

The grey sedan leapt into airport traffic from the curb, belching vapor from its tailpipe, and Katrina looked around. Saturday morning travelers bunched up around curbside kiosks with luggage in tow, but Katrina wouldn't be checking any bags—not today—and now Petrova's voice was in her ear again.

"You're being watched, love."

"I know. In motion," Katrina whispered.

Katrina's blonde hair, svelte figure, and green eyes normally got a second glance, but not now. The black wig, sunglasses, and shopping bags had transformed her, and the stares from men had vanished. She only hoped the disguise would delay the NYPD and FBI, because she was sure to be run through NCIC after the surveillance was pulled.

The sound of high heels echoed on the sidewalk as announcements sounded overhead. She moved into international departures with confidently swaying hips, then ascended an escalator. A sharp pain shot through her right hand, but she held onto the shopping bag until she reached the top. She dropped the load at the landing and winced in pain, then looked at her glove, which was crimson where her blood had soaked through.

The shopping bag handles were reinforced with wire to carry the load, but Petrova had used too thin a gauge. The bag's weight caused the handles to cut into Katrina's flesh like razors, but the discomfort was minor, and the small sacrifice felt good.

The expanse of the international terminal surprised her, and she looked up like a tourist. The soaring expanse was over a hundred feet high and sunlight striped the interior like the crisscross of pastry dough on a pie. A digital clock reminded Katrina of Sumito and his schedule, and she felt her anger grow. Her thoughts about him were unimportant, but it was hard to control her disdain for the talkative financier.

Hundreds of travelers were queued up at check-in counters on the concourse below, but she favored a detour, wending her way down a corridor on the mezzanine. She arrived outside the operations center of a certain airline and glanced at the company's logo and glass double-doors. Dozens of pilots and crew were inside collecting assignments and reports for their day's work. She moved closer to the glass and saw the laughter and smiles on people's faces, and someone caught her eye. She turned quickly and headed back in the direction she had come.

On the concourse, the same carrier's logo caught her eye, with its intertwined purple arches and falcon in flight: RASH Airlines. The carrier's agents were busy working their queue and Katrina slunk by.

Her shopping bag came to rest between the airline's counter and an exit, and the sound of ripping paper was in the air. One of her shopping bags vanished—or so it seemed—and a brown briefcase stood in its place. She pivoted on her heels and whispered into her microphone.

"A bird with a broken wing can't fly," she said.

"The future looks bloody," said Petrova.

"Not now, Pet."

"Very bloody."

"Petrova, please! Radio discipline." The terminal's moving walkway hastened Katrina's exit to AirTrain and her earpiece crackled.

"You worry too much, love."

"And you talk too much."

AirTrain slid away from international departures, and Katrina looked out onto JFK operations. Flat gray light painted service vehicles, tankers, and jets in two dimensions like pieces of a collage. Her thoughts went to the team.

Katrina's main concern was Petrova, because the young Hillingdon girl was too green to be so arrogant. She was cocksure without experience to back it up. In fact, Petrova's only bona fides were in surveillance and communications—hardly a coup for a team that depended on diverse skill sets.

The train slipped along the elevated rails, making its stops and sounding announcements overhead. Finally, a chime rang out and the doors flung open at Howard Beach, where Katrina joined the departing throng for the subway terminus.

"We're at 256-bit encryption, love. Safe from those who listen and those who wish Edward Snowden a Colombian necktie," Petrova said.

"In motion, Pet."

The remaining shopping bag came to rest outside the disabled exit gate at the subway entrance. Katrina feigned confusion, fumbling in her purse, and when she looked up the shopping bag was gone. A bundle covered in fast food wrappers was at her feet.

"Second delivery," Katrina whispered into her mic.

"Your new hairdo suits you, love. Brunette is very 'girl next door.' Every man wants a girl next door. *Oooh! Oooh!* Guess who else loved brunettes with long straight hair?" Petrova let out a little yelp over the radio and Katrina found her reflection in a vending machine.

"I'm *this* close to turning you off," Katrina said.

"Serial killer Ted Bundy. Every one of the thirty girls he butchered had long straight dark hair parted in the middle." Katrina smoothed her wig with the palm of her hand. "Even serial killers want a brunette—to decapitate," Petrova said. Katrina checked her lipstick in the shiny reflection and wriggled in her skirt.

"They talk about female empowerment, but I don't buy it. We're supposed to have our careers and 'be women,' whatever that means. Being a woman is a bitch. Besides, the camera adds ten pounds," Petrova snorted. " You're going to look like a fat pig in the surveillance!"

"For god's sake, stop talking!" Katrina said.

"Sumito wants a word with you, Kat."

The sound of Katrina's footsteps echoed over the radio.

"Kat? *Hello?* He needs to talk with you."

"In motion, Pet."

"Talk with him, OK?"

"No more comms. See you at the RV. Out."

The flow of commuters slowed and Katrina found herself in a rare moment, alone at the Howard Beach subway entrance. She swiped her MetroCard and bustled through the gates to discover two men and a dog standing against a far wall with no one else in sight. The men wore dark blue clothing emblazoned with big yellow block letters: NYPD.

She catalogued their kits in the blink of an eye: body armor, 9mm pistols, protective glasses, helmets, gloves, encrypted radios, and lace-up boots. *These aren't precinct cops*, she mused, and then she saw the shadows at their sides: submachine guns. *Fuck.* It was CountTer, the NYPD Strategic Response Group's counter terrorism unit.

And yet there was a small grace note, because the cops had with them not a Labrador but a German Shepherd. Shepherds didn't have the refined sense of smell for anti-terror work. In fact, German Shepherds couldn't sniff out bombs to save their furry little lives. The saying was true: *Labs blab but the Germans will get you.*

She quieted her steps and reduced the arc of her swinging arms to be less noticeable, trying to blend into the background even as her wig shined underneath the walkway's mercury-vapor lights. But there was only one way to the A train to Queens—directly into the line of sight of New York City's elite anti-terror unit.

The sound of high heels echoed on the breezeway, and the police stirred like cheetahs at a watering hole hearing a lone gazelle. The police dog stood up and the men turned in her direction, and Katrina froze. The sound of central dispatch squawked over the police radios and the moment hung in the air with each party aware of the other...and then Katrina moved.

She pivoted toward the men, smiled, then did a little schoolgirl wave. *You fat fucks,* she thought. Her heels clicked and she turned for the Queens platform and didn't look back. *Tick, tick, tick, motherfuckers.*

She knew she'd been made, but it wasn't by the cops. The surveillance system of cameras, radiation detectors, and chemical sensors in the train station was the more likely culprit. The system was in nearly all U.S. transit hubs and it stood to reason she'd already been hoovered up and stored on hard disk.

Katrina's start with Sumito's team had been very much by the book when she'd put out her shingle in Hillingdon those months ago. She announced her availability using the standard euphemisms, crafting her ad like a clever copywriter: "Freelance contractor specialising in hard-to-complete assignments," the headline read. She included phrases like "detail oriented under extreme pressure," and "ability to achieve objectives under high stress with a highly evolved tool set." She could "travel immediately for domestic and foreign assignments." Of course.

Having introduced herself through the usual London channels, she waited anxiously for a bite. It wasn't long before Sumito responded and the forced smiles and fake compliments at Highlands Park told her she'd gotten the job. She would be part of a small team leaving London for New York very soon.

The work would be distasteful, she knew, but it wasn't the job that had her stomach churning. The more she talked to Sumito, the more she felt her disdain grow. First, there was his ugly halitosis, which was compounded by his preference for close talking and the spittle that routinely shot from his lips.

Sumito's lack of hygiene made Katrina bristle, and yet anything was better than being on the dole in the land of fog and marmalade. She'd spent too much time feeling envious of her friends who were jetting off for adventures in far-flung places. She would stick out this assignment, resolved not to let Sumito bother her.

She descended the escalator to the platform, clutching her purse tight, and didn't look back to the mezzanine. But there was still the matter of the final device that would trigger the chain reaction. More importantly, it would shoot sparks twenty feet in the air like a Fourth of July firework and scare the daylights out of the commuters. She only hoped the device would fit through one of the trash cans' openings. Of course, the device wasn't dangerous. It was only there to funnel people to the exit, where they'd be greeted by the exploding construction nails.

Sumito's plan was of no small concern, and in fact, he'd micromanaged every detail. The result was a nit-picking of Katrina's work, and the two had nearly come to blows during many heated discussions. Sumito wanted bloodshed, whereas Katrina didn't think violence was the best way to start a conversation.

Katrina imagined commuters stacked at the exit struggling to get out like clubgoers trying to flee a nightclub fire. She thought of the screams and cries for help, how the explosion would shred flesh from bone, and the children who would certainly die. And yet she'd already placed the terminal device. What was the use of feelings now?

She thought back to Sumito's late-night monologues as they studied maps and rehearsed their roles. She remembered him staring at her silently for hours as they did their work, how he would invade her personal space and make her anxious. She thought of his constant critiques and felt queasy.

Her stomach churned like a boat on a stormy sea. She grabbed a column for support, trying to catch her breath. Her stomach lurched again and she doubled over, vomiting onto the platform. She grabbed her thighs as her face contorted and then threw up again as people around her scattered. She hugged the column, groaning, then wiped her mouth and continued walking.

The platform was packed with people, but there was a sliver of privacy by the station elevator and she slid a hand inside her purse to feel for the device. Her finger was on the safety as she walked toward a trash can a few yards away, then depressed the countdown timer.

There was a hand on her arm and she jumped.

"No way!" a girl yelled, grabbing onto Katrina and screaming excitedly. The teenager was wearing shorts and an I ♥ NY T-shirt and held onto Katrina's forearm like a vice grip. "Oh my god. Oh my god! It's you!" she said, jumping up and down. "You're the host of *Fresh Looks and Fun Facts*, amiright!?"

"No, no. No!" Katrina shook her head and pulled her arm away.

"Mom! Dad! It's *her*. It's the girl I was telling you about from the show!" The teen was hot on Katrina's heels as a train horn blared in the distance. The horn sounded again as the train entered the station, then zipped past the platform without stopping.

Petrova would be waiting for her at the RV, and together, they would change clothes and meet up with Sumito at the safe house—that was the plan.

There was a screech of metal on metal as another train arrived at the platform. Air brakes hissed loudly as the train stopped and the doors flung open. The crowd surged, pinning Katrina against a pillar so she couldn't move.

"See!" the girl said to her parents as she pointed at Katrina. "She's from the show I was telling you about!" The family turned and examined Katrina like a lab specimen. "I'd recognize you anywhere!" the girl said.

"No! No! You have the wrong person!" Katrina struggled to move. The crowd swirled around them while the timer counted down.

3

THE TRAFFIC ON NINTH AVENUE is moving, but the sidewalks are clogged like a blood vessel with arterial plaque. Restaurant touts are the chief contributors to the log jam, calling out to tourists with al fresco dining options.

"Puppy!" says a voice behind me.

Plim speeds toward me from 45th Street with a big smile, and I already feel better. Her arms wrap around me, and there's a kiss on my cheek and a mop of curly hair in my face as she presses into my shoulder.

"Puppy, it's so good to see you. I've been on the phone to like *everyone*," she says.

"That feels so good. Could you hold me some more?" Her hands caress my back and shoulders again and I sigh.

"It's OK," Plim says, rubbing me.

"I'm a little lonely."

"I heard about the takeoff, but I don't know exactly what happened to you guys," she says.

The door to Scandino's opens, and before I know it, we're being seated outside. I can't believe she got us a reservation—and on a Thursday evening no less—not that I have much of an appetite. The outdoor patio is already filled with diners. We sit.

"I should be back in the cockpit in less than a week. Thank god. They call it 'administrative leave,' but I'll be back!" I say.

"Good, I'm so glad to hear it," Plim says.

"We over-rotated on the roll. A tail strike happens to a carrier at least once or twice a year. You return to the airport, maintenance does a damage check, and you're on your way. But we had significant damage, like the flight that hit the light stanchions on takeoff and tore through its belly."

"Sounds scary," Plim says.

"I don't know...Could you...could you...I mean...Can I come over?" I stand and walk over to her chair and sit like a golden retriever. "Could you hold me again?"

She embraces me from the side and her warm arms encircle my chest and shoulders. Her fingers interlock in a hug around me, and I'm adrift on a calm sea. My eyes close as I realize that this is her superpower. When she holds me like this, all of my problems go away and my facade cracks like a cheap veneer.

"You're sad, puppy. Please stop worrying, Clay. You'll be OK, I promise." Her hands are on my face, and her fingers trace the creases that line my cheeks and eyes. "Here's where the sad is," she says.

"Those are wrinkles!" I laugh and move closer to her as a tear rolls down my cheek.

"Your baseline is sad, puppy."

"I know!" I laugh some more. There's softness on my forehead as her lips press against my skin in a kiss.

"I'm here for you, puppy. Always."

I don't understand pure affection like this because all of my defenses come down when she holds me. I feel good in the moment, but when she lets go, my sadness returns like the tide, and I have to make peace with my melancholy.

"You have no idea how good that felt."

"It was just a hug," she says.

"The whole world is different. It changed everything," I say, wiping my face and sitting back down.

"It's OK."

"Take a look at this," I say, holding out my phone. She takes one glance at the screen and waves it away with a hand, and I grimace. "*What?*"

"Tell me what it says."

"It's exactly the type of job I've been looking for. It's not perfect, but it's—"

"Read it to me, OK?" Plim says.

"Sure." I clear my throat and read from the screen:

WE ARE AN INTERNATIONALLY RECOGNISED
COMPANY PROUD TO ANNOUNCE A NEW
COMMERCIAL AVIATION PROGRAMME. WE INVITE
QUALIFIED PILOTS TO JOIN OUR NETWORK AS WE
REVOLUTIONISE AVIATION IN SEVERAL
COUNTRIES. WE ARE SEEKING SENIOR CAPTAINS
FOR ROUTES IN NORTH AMERICA, EUROPE,
NORTH AFRICA, AND THE MIDDLE EAST.
CANDIDATES WITH TYPE-RATED A319/A320/A321

AND B777/B787 AIRCRAFT SPECIALISATIONS ARE
INVITED TO JOIN OUR ELITE CORPS. CANDIDATES
MUST HAVE 5,000 HOURS AS PIC AND 7,000 HOURS
TFT WITH 2,000 HOURS TURBINE PIC. COMPETITIVE
SALARY AND BENEFITS. RELOCATION AVAILABLE.
ARE YOU READY TO CLIMB TO THE NEXT ALTITUDE
OF YOUR CAREER? LET'S FLY.

HTTPS://JRTYHELMENTRXY.ONION/CAREERS

"I'm definitely going to apply." She's gazing at the avenue with her head in her hand. "It's gotta be a British carrier: 'recognised, programme.' And if it's European, they've got crazy-good benefits and better hours. But it's not the best part...I'd be a senior captain, Plim! I could start building a real life in New York." She's still looking out to the street. "Plim?"

"Hmmm?...Sorry."

"What are you...what's wrong?" I say.

"I'm relieved you're OK. After what happened to you and Matt last week, I..." Her hand is now on mine. "Puppy, I'm glad you guys made it back. I don't know what I would've done if you'd—"

"Stop. And please don't call me puppy. I would've texted you from the hotel, but you know, RASH S.O.P. No outbound communications allowed after an incident."

"I know. Standard operating procedure." She takes her hand away and looks back to the avenue.

"I really need one of the senior captain spots at RASH or this British airline. I hope the incident hasn't derailed my plans. Onward! So, what's it like being the only retired lesbian type-rated captain in Manhattan? You must be the only one on the island!"

"Gay is the only calling card I need, Clay. We're 10% of NYC, 50% of Chelsea, and 100% of female volleyball coaches." She laughs.

Her face crinkles, and the lines on her face remind me why I like her so much. Everything about her is genuine, and her gray hair and latte complexion only add to her beauty.

"Admit it, Plim, you miss being a RASHer. Armored cockpit doors, wind shear, unlimited pretzel nuggets."

"You really know how to sell it!" She huffs and puts her napkin in her lap as the waiter arrives to take our order. The smell of roasted garlic and baking bread is in the air and blankets the patio like a cloud. The heavenly scent teases the food to come, but I'm just happy being with her. And now I'm looking at my feet.

"Something on your mind?" she says.

"No. I don't think so...No."

"Are you sad, Clay? It's OK."

"I'm always sad."

"It'll be OK, I promise...Retirement's treating me well. Randala and I are two happy clams," she says. "Get it? *Clams*?"

"Even you can't make that funny. You just earned a demerit from the lesbian pun oversight committee." She sticks out her tongue at me.

"When Randala's not lawyering, we're homebodies, you know? Reading books, TV–"

"Please tell me you guys watch *Jill Parabola, US Air Marshal*?!" I say.

"Damn straight! We never miss it," she says, and we laugh. "We read to each other and–" She reacts to my expression. "Sorry, I didn't mean to make you jealous."

"Yes, I'm jealous! Who doesn't want a good woman?" I say.

"To good women!" Plim says, raising her glass.

"To good women!" She grabs some bread, her shoulders hunch, and she starts coughing.

"I don't care about skirt chasing and the whole senior captain lifestyle. I want to grow a life where my career doesn't dictate everything. You can't invest in yourself when you're always on call and have to leave at a moment's notice and–"

Plim's still coughing. "Are you OK?" My expression turns to worry. "God! Are you choking!?"

I move to her with my Heimlich at the ready, and she points at my chair like a schoolmarm. I plop in my seat, fold my arms across my chest, and watch the coughing continue.

"That doesn't sound good. It sounds like...you know what it sounds like? It sounds like a respiratory infection. You should really get it looked at." I lean back in my chair, confident in my diagnosis, and wait. She clears her throat, sips some water, and catches my look.

"It's OK. It's nothing," she says.

"It's *not* nothing, and I know that for a fact."

"It's OK, Clay. Stop worrying. Are you afraid I'm going to die?" There's a sharp laugh from her like a bark.

"See? *That!* It sounds like a seal's bark. And don't get all macabre with me. I hate when you do that—I need you here with me. You're important on my journey," I say.

"On your *journey*? Awww. That's so cute, puppy. You're always so serious. It's only death. I'm not afraid of dying as long as there's wine on earth. Wine makes everything better."

"Please don't do this to me. You're my only friend...You and HazMatt. I don't have anyone else."

"I'm fine. Be here with me now," Plim says and touches my hand. "I'm good." Warmth radiates through my soul as her skin touches mine.

"It feels so good, but I don't understand it. Your touch is comforting because I'm lonely for female touch and I don't have anyone who loves me. And the fact you're not interested in me doesn't make your touch any less sweet. It feels like love and I'm confused. Why am I here with you when I could be with a *real woman*!?" It's then I realize what I've said. "Oh god. I'm sorry. That was cruel."

"You do need a *real woman*!" she says, laughing, and now we're both laughing.

"Why does it feel good when you touch me even though there's no romance?" I say. A soft whimper is in the air.

"Because you need to get laid, Clay. *Poo-say* makes everything better, and you can take that from a professional...and what's that sound you're making, puppy? Please don't worry. I had some cough medicine earlier today and I'm good. Honestly, it's a cough."

There's the sound of chairs scraping on concrete, and a family is seated next to us. The foursome has two young girls with curly hair in identical tank dresses with colored stripes and white sandals.

"Awww...they look so sweet," I say as a napkin rises to my eyes.

Plim smiles at the family, too. "Very sweet...It's OK, puppy. You know who's fine? This retired type-rated lesbian jet captain." We both laugh. "To be honest, I've never felt better."

"Your cough doesn't sound right, and your wife probably wants you to get it checked, too."

"Randala knows I can take care of a 700 thousand pound airliner as well as a cough. You always get freaked out, Clay. Be calm."

"I'm worried. Please get it checked, OK?"

"Tell me about the takeoff," she says.

"I missed Matt's callout because I passed out and he had to take over. I was OK at pushback and—"

"How's he holding up?"

"My last medical said I was good...Matt's pissed. I'm going to see him soon. We have to wait for the final report, but for now I'm on paid leave pending the investigation." There's the sound of footsteps behind me and a voice humming a tune I don't know.

"Here you guys go! One margherita!" the waiter says, setting down our pie. The pizza steams like a manhole cover in wintertime, and a pile of napkins lands next to me. "Enjoy!"

Circles of buffalo mozzarella commingle with splotches of tangy red tomato sauce, garlic, basil, and olive oil. The golden brown crust glistens with oil.

"Come to papa," I say, hoisting a slice. The crust, sauce, and cheese melt on my tongue in perfect harmony. "Ridiculous," I say, uttering sounds of pleasure. "And hot, hot, *hot*!" The slice drops to my plate, and I make huffing noises.

"What's the latest on the girl front?"

"*God.* Must we do this?" I say.

"We must."

"OK. Later...Can we talk about the British carrier? If RASH won't promote me based on the tail strike, I'll need to go elsewhere. I want to grow my career in a place that will nurture me. I want my needs to be considered."

"All I'm hearing is 'I want,' but it's a job, Clay. It's not designed to fulfill your every need. You've got a good job at RASH, and switching carriers will be stressful. Nobody's going to take care of you except *you*."

Plim picks up her phone and the light colors her face in an eerie blue glow. She scratches her cheek, brushes back her hair, and works the device with both hands.

"I finally have the seniority for a senior captain spot, but I'm not sure I'll get it—the company rarely promotes from within. But applying for a new job sucks because I'll have to do everything again: interviews, simulator evaluation, background check, substance abuse screening. At least I have type-rated experience on the jets they want," I say.

"A bigger title means more stress," Plim says. "You may have *less* time for yourself and the things you want. What if you become senior captain and it takes more of your time?"

"Why are you being such a downer?" I say.

"What am I supposed to say? That all of your problems are going to disappear at a new carrier? A job isn't supposed to be fun. That's why they call it *work*."

"I hope I get reinstated. A black mark would ruin my career anywhere."

"So..." she says with a rising tone. "Who's the girl *du jour*? Is it Kelli who handwrites her name by dotting her *i* with a little heart? Or, is it Amberh, the girl whose name ends with a silent *h*? Wait! I know! It's another damaged girl you found online."

"You're cruel. And for the record, I liked Kelli and Amberh, but there were issues."

"Issues, huh?" Plim laughs. "But you still dated them!" She uses her fingers to make air quotes around the word *dated*.

"Ha-ha. I want one woman."

"Your online profile should say, 'Needy airline pilot seeks love and affection. Obsessed with action films and dental hygiene.'" She laughs.

"The truth hurts. It hurts."

I don't think Plim's assessment of my romantic life is accurate—I date a diverse set of women: sexy and conservative, quiet and loud, cheap and spendy, foreign and domestic. And yet there's one thing about the women I date that's true: they're damaged.

I rush to damaged women like a paramedic, taking stock of their emotional and psychological wounds, then triage them to locate their pain. My goal is to help them through what ails them and get them to the therapist's couch. I want them to ditch the booze, drugs, binge eating, hookups, excessive spending, and self-harm.

And no, I don't ask for details on their strife because it saddles my spirit. Call me selfish if you want, but I have enough of my own demons to contend with—I don't need any more. It's not that I'm insensitive to their problems, but I can't bear the weight of too much sadness. Their stories of divorce, abuse, violence, poverty, addiction, trauma, or suicide are too much to handle.

"Your whole 'helping' thing is a facade. Window dressing," Plim says.

"Come on."

"You say you want to help these girls, but you never do. Things start out hot and heavy and grow serious, but then you bail on them because of issues. Of course there are issues. That's why you chose them! You need help, Clay."

"I'm working on myself, and I like taking care of people. What's wrong with that?"

What Plim doesn't realize is that my desires come from a place of concern and have nothing to do with me being messed up in the head.

"Let's not argue, OK?" she says. "I want to take Randala to India. Can you get us a friends and family fare next month? She's wrapping up a case, and I want to take her to Kolkata to volunteer. Be nice to do something good," she says.

"I've changed, Plim. I'm different now."

"India, Clay."

"I've done the work on myself and I'm changing."

"A Boeing is a Boeing is a Boeing," she says.

"Ouch...You love me and then you hurt me," I say. She laughs.

"The trip, Clay. Can you get us tickets?"

"I'll look into it. India for two. I'll check into fares and..." I raise my eyebrows and smile. "Any chance you want company?"

Plim laughs. "*You?* Volunteering with the poor?"

"Yes, me. Don't act so surprised. I could do it. I'm on hiatus, and I've got nothing else going on."

"*You?* With us? In India," she says.

"*What?!*"

"I can't imagine you, Mr. Squeamish, in India."

"Come on," I say.

"There are no swanky hotels, no swim-up bars, no in-room massages," she says, making air quotes around the word *massages*.

"Hilarious. I've done turns to India before, Plim," I say.

"No bikini girls sucking on Blow Pops lounging by the pool."

"Of course not...What flavor Blow Pops?"

I can almost see her air-thumbing the 900+ page DSM-V, hunting for my mental health problems and diagnostic codes. In Plim's mind, I'm not sensitive but pathologic, shacking up with these women until another young thing walks by. But that's not me at all. In fact, it's usually the women I date who break things off first.

I find needy women attractive because they cherish and greet me with a smile. They help me ditch my unhealthy impulses by showing me something worth doing. But my helping cycles are enervating, and I realize I can't put a Band-Aid on the world.

I look up from my ruminating to find Plim nibbling on a slice of pizza and looking at me with those brown eyes.

"What?" she says.

"You *sure* you guys don't want company in India?" I say, smiling.

4

A SPORTY EXHAUST NOTE IS in the air as I slalom between traffic and calculate each vehicle's vector like an air traffic controller. The roar pours out of my machine like a sports car, ricocheting off the buildings on Atlantic Avenue.

Vrooms and roars thrill me. They are the reason I ride and, yes, I know how that must sound—weird, quirky, a little juvenile. But I've come to accept my sonic kink and I feel lucky because my baby is a 1000cc Chigasaki and she caresses my ear just right.

The last time I saw Matt was at Hotel Nowhere, the RASH Airlines crash pad. The Nowhere is the place RASH puts you up when they want you alone. It sits on Queens Boulevard between a sushi joint and a railway bridge. Matt and I were escorted to the Nowhere after the JFK incident—and by "escorted," I mean we were ordered there by the RASH brass.

Just calling the Nowhere a hotel is a stretch because it has no bar or restaurant, no lobby or front desk staff. There's nothing out front to welcome you, except a sign with the words DISCOUNT FURNITURE to discourage passersby. Even the rooms are bare bones, with only a bed and metal dresser, making the Nowhere about as comfortable as a minimum-security prison.

The traffic light ahead changes from green to yellow and then red, so I ease up on the gas and downshift. The engine rumbles as I drag my boots along the ground and roll to a stop. A breeze cools me through the vents in my jacket, and the sun is low in the sky.

Matt and I were separated at the Nowhere, then ushered into separate suites where RASH brass and FAA investigators were waiting. We had to turn in our pilot licenses, provide urine and blood samples, and *then* we got questioned.

I was nervous because of stories I'd heard about investigators running roughshod over pilot rights. Good pilots had lost their jobs to investigators with hard-ons for fly boys in incidents those pilots had no control over: computer crashes, mechanical failures, weather. No pilot wanted to lose their job and end up the chump in the orange vest at the local home improvement store. HOW MAY I OFFER YOU EXCELLENT SERVICE TODAY? Forget that. Matt and I wouldn't go down without a fight.

The traffic light overhead sways in the breeze like a sock on a clothesline, and the avenue's quiet. My idle sounds better than I remember and I realize how much I missed my girl—the Chigasaki. I twist the throttle, she roars, and I rev her again to delight in her sonic cries. There's a vibration in my pocket that tells me Matt's probably at the café.

RASH Airlines has its issues like any other carrier, but our biggest problem is the silverbacks—the senior captains. They sit at the top of the pilot hierarchy and muscle their way around like a troop of silverback gorillas with little grace or consequence. And their favorite move is the schedule flip.

A schedule flip is a route change that maximizes a silverback's lifestyle without the distasteful aspects of a flying career. These schedule changes are mostly used for skirt chasing, but can also be used to skip bad turns or toxic pilots. It's a work optimization strategy so the senior captains only have to fly where and when they want.

Maybe a silverback has found a girl in a foreign city he wants to woo and needs a few days to close the deal—so he flips schedules. Or maybe he wants to avoid a double turn to Dulles (that's NYC → IAD → NYC → IAD → NYC) or a layover in Dayton or Managua. Or, he's had a bad encounter with a first officer (F.O.) and doesn't want a reprise.

So, the silverback calls up RASH flight operations and, really, his excuse is no different from what everybody uses: cold/flu, food poisoning, plumbing emergency, medical appointment, childcare problem, death of a relative, or ill parent. And like that, he's removed from his route and a junior captain is slotted in his place.

I like to give our silverbacks the benefit of the doubt when they flip schedules because I figure their excuses may have some merit. Skirt chasing is one thing, but the senior captain's beef may be legitimate, like wanting to avoid an F.O. who isn't up to snuff.

And flying with a bad F.O. is no day at the pier with candy and ice cream—it means being stuck with an addict, doofus, or bully at 33,000 feet. You definitely don't want them touching any instruments or making any decisions in the air because, well, it's bad for your health. The best case scenario is the F.O. falls asleep before takeoff, and the worst case is too frightening to fathom. Flying next to a bad F.O. is like flying next to a can of gasoline casually smoking a cigarette.

The silverback knows full well that his schedule flip will ripple across the RASH system and screw *someone*. He knows that a junior captain will have to grit their teeth as they're told the news: *Enjoy your weekend in San Salvador!* or *Good luck with your triple turn to Philly next week!*

The traffic light turns green. I launch off the line, pouring it on, and I know this is as good as it gets. The Chigasaki responds instantly to my inputs and shifting weight. I'm having a blast until the traffic slows suddenly. I lean right and split the lanes to swallow up a few more blocks.

I like to do a little research when I'm called up from the bench to replace a silverback. I'll look him up in the RASH database and on social media to get a sense of the man. I'll read his posts and bio, click on his pics, and imagine what he's really doing on his day off. *He's probably in a foreign city right now with a young girl*, I'll think, and I'll envision the lie that launched his escapade.

I imagine him calling up our flight operations group, hacking into the phone like an Academy Award winner. It's not just a cold and cough, he says, but aches and chills, nausea and vomiting. *You know, I should stay in bed the next few days,* he says.

Of course, he's really in Miami or Rio or Roppongi with some paid talent, a blister pack of boner pills by his side, light streaming through the curtains of his bar district motel room. The phone glows against his cheek until he's done telling his lies and then he tosses the handset aside. He pulls the girl closer, kissing her, and his smile grows a mile wide—and why shouldn't it? He's living the dream of commercial aviation, and I admire him for it. He grabs the girl and they make love again as the ceiling fan swims in slow motion like a carousel in the sky.

I ease off the throttle and brake as I roll up on another red light, flipping my sun visor and squeezing the clutch so I can give her some gas. She rumbles like an idling rocket as I watch the signal overhead. The light turns green, and I pop the clutch, launching us off the line.

A bus enters the fast lane, cutting me off, then meanders between the lanes like a snake impeding all westbound traffic. Our mini putt-putt parade inches along as the bus belches smoke and sounds its one-note flatulence. Finally, he moves right and I pour it on, devouring a few more blocks.

Downtown is up ahead so I ease off the gas to make out the addresses...*425, 483, 497.* I slow down and look for parking, then find a sliver of open space and duck-walk the bike into a slot between two parked cars. I kill the engine and realize how quiet the avenue is, with birds chirping in the trees outside the café.

• • •

Adorable twenty- and thirtysomethings are huddled up front, cuddling cups of coffee and waiting to be seated. Meanwhile, waiters work the tables with brisk efficiency like airport ground crews, delivering a steady stream of caffeine and carbs to the well-coiffed patrons.

It looks like Brooklyn has come down with a case of bed head, judging by the amount of disheveled hairstyles here. The unkempt look is the currency of cool Brooklyn youth and means *I'm chill, bro.* You don't put effort into your hair here, because "effort" is the antithesis of cool and vanity is frowned upon.

The hostess gives me a once-over in her role as sentry, and I pantomime that I know where I'm going, so she lets me pass into the seating area. Matt sits next to a window overlooking the patio, face buried in his phone.

"Bring it in," I say with a smile.

"No thanks. I'm not in the mood for a man-hug."

"What's wrong?" It's then I notice his dour expression. "You know what? Never–"

"What did I *just* say, Clay? This isn't about you and your needs," Matt says.

I sigh, then sit, as a waitress swings by with menus to take our drink orders. I lean back and realize that Matt's fitness regimen has done him well, giving him more upper body definition with thicker shoulders and arms.

"There's nothing wrong with male friendship," I say.

"I'm not interested in you, Clay, and you're not interested in me. You need a woman—or are you coming out to me?"

"Be chill, HazMatt. It was a hug, not a kiss."

There's the clanging of silverware next to us as a couple nearby receive a plate of French toast piled high with berries and powdered sugar. The dish lands between them and I can already feel the carb pangs gnawing at my stomach.

"Clay, you're the most gay-acting straight dude I've ever met. No one else talks about feelings and friendship all day like you do. You know who *else* thinks you're gay?" Matt says.

I stare at him blankly.

"Gay dudes," he says.

Most of the diners are couples. I realize Matt and I also look like companions, with our fashion choices synchronized from over a decade of working together—polo shirts, jeans, tech watches, and reading glasses for me, sunglasses for Matt. Our body language mimics each other from all the time spent working side by side.

"This couldn't come at a worse time. I was about to submit my application for senior captain and I'm not sure I–"

"What's this '*I*' shit? We both lost our licenses because of something *you* did," he says.

"Everything at the Nowhere went as well as it could've. They're going through our statements and congratulations are–"

"*Congratulations?*" Matt says.

"Yeah. RASH brass liked how we did with the FAA."

"What?"

"What do you mean, 'What,' Matt? The brass liked how we handled ourselves," I say.

"How we *handled ourselves?*" Matt says, setting his gaze on me.

"Got a hearing problem? Yes, you did a great job. You–"

"You can't put lipstick on a turd, Clay."

"It's 'lipstick on a pig.'"

"Whatever," Matt says. I stare at him silently and think of another line of conversation.

"I know you're angry about the incident. I passed out and don't know why. My last medical said I was in perfect health and my doctor–"

"I don't give a *fuck* what your doctor said! Be straight with me, because this is about the cockpit voice, isn't it?

You want to crash so you can hear the cockpit computer voice like Sam Varsick," Matt says.

"No! I don't want to die." I look him in the eye. "My medical report said I was–" Matt looks at me unsatisfied. "I'm not trying to kill myself."

"Anything else you wanna tell me?" Matt says.

"Like what? That I'm drinking, drugging, banging whores? Tell me what you want to hear," I say.

A busboy arrives with waters. Matt spits out his gum and sends a text while I extract the lemon wedge from my drink. Dark clouds hang over the patio.

"Nobody cares about Sam Varsick, Clay. He's a tired old silverback," Matt says.

"He's got history at RASH and he's been around the block. Maybe he could give me some advice. Help me get my career back on track so I can apply for senior captain," I say.

"I wouldn't believe anything from that sick fuck," Matt says.

"He's been at RASH forever."

"Come on, Clay. Varsick is an unstable hothead. It's a miracle he's still with the company." Matt sighs loudly as rain drops start to sprinkle the patio and diners move to find shelter underneath the awnings.

"The news is making me sick," Matt says.

"Don't worry about the headlines. News has a short lifespan. There's always another item that'll bump the incident off the radar. You have to be patient," I say.

"The number one search result for your name is the incident," Matt says.

"What?"

"Mine, too," he says.

"*Shit.*"

"We're being tried in the court of public opinion, Clay. Not you. *Me.* The press blames me for what happened. My girlfriend comes home every night in tears because of the nasty comments people are posting online."

"Like?"

"It's evil," Matt says.

"There's this top-secret building in Russia where hundreds of people are paid to manipulate online opinion twenty-four hours a day. Their targets vary from products and services to people and corporations, but their method is the same: lies and disinformation," I say.

"My girlfriend found an online article about us with an illustration of a RASH jet sitting on a debris-strewn runway. The plane's tail was attached to the jet with plastic tape. There was a caricature of me in the cockpit, and the headline read, *Is Your Pilot Any Good?* People in the comments section were saying stuff like, 'I wouldn't let Matt Blancando clean up after my dog' and 'I hope his son gets leukemia.' Who are these sickos?"

"It's called depersonalization, HazMatt."

He raises his eyebrows at me.

"Our digital devices create a feeling of detachment because we feel safe behind our screens. We're hidden and it allows us to spew hatred online. Nobody believes online comments." I fold my arms over my chest, and Matt shoots me another look.

"Sure they do. They think more posts means there's a kernel of truth," he says.

"Everything online is for sale. Social proof can be gamed. Any outcome can be had," I say.

"What?"

"Manipulation is easy. Online truth is an oxymoron," I say.

"Are you doing a term paper or something? My life is being destroyed one comment at a time," he says.

Rain is falling steadily on the patio as busboys rush to and fro clearing dishware from the tables. Damp diners have already squeezed inside the cavernous restaurant, crowding the entryway more.

"Let time run its course," I say.

"Easy for you to say. The crosshairs aren't on your chest. Who writes an essay for an online comment?" A waitress arrives with our coffees, and I wriggle on the hard wooden chair, trying to get comfortable.

"They're sock puppets—fake digital users, HazMatt. They go to work whenever something's at stake: money, fame, celebrity, politics. There are thousands of fake accounts on every popular website and social network and they're used to pump up products, people, services, agendas. All you need is a stack of virtual credit cards and fake email addresses to create an online consensus about anything. Or, create a fictional crowd to destroy your enemies online. They call those digital death squads," I say.

"How do you know about this?" Matt says.

"I hear about these things."

"It's crowdsourced character assassination," Matt says furrowing his brow.

"Except there's no crowd."

The waitress arrives and I take charge, ordering oatmeal for Matt, an egg white omelet for me, and fresh-squeezed orange juice for us both. I smile and place the order like a knowing spouse and discover a smile on Matt's face.

"You remembered, sweetie!" he says.

"Of course, honey!"

"Oh, honey!" Matt laughs. It's the first smile for either of us today. I fiddle with my fork and wonder if there's anything I can say to comfort him.

"The good news is the news cycle changes hourly, buddy boy."

"I can't compete with the online lies, but I want people to know who I really am," he says.

"I know who you are, and your friends do, too. That's what matters."

"The web is where people go to research people they know or want to meet, and that's what sucks. You can't control it, and yet it controls your destiny...This is my career, Clay, which means I don't have a fallback." His phone is now in his hand, and he is searching for something.

"Everyone will know what happened when the review board is done with their inquiry, Matt. The flying public has a short atten—" I say.

"One person online wrote, 'The copilot nearly killed everyone because RASH Airlines doesn't train copilots as well as pilots. The copilot made several mistakes after the pilot had a medical emergency,'" Matt says. There's fury on his face as he looks up at me.

"There's no such thing as a 'copilot!' I'm a first officer and both of us are equally skilled at flying. So it's like this? I save everyone after you pass out, and yet I'm the jackass while you're the pilot with the heart of gold? Fuck that," he says.

"Calm down. I know that's how it looks, but—" I say as he reads another item off his phone.

"Someone else wrote, 'I was a RASH Airlines flight attendant for over a decade and supported them when they were a young carrier. I believed in our service back then, but I quit this year because RASH has turned into an ultra-discount carrier and cuts corners to save money. My husband and I took a trip on RASH from Palm Springs and our flight's engine failed. On another nonstop to Cancun for our anniversary, we skidded off the runway on the return to Palm Springs. I won't fly them. Never,'" Matt says, reading from the screen.

He looks up and me. "These are lies, Clay. RASH has never served Palm Springs or Cancun! These are lies to get people to turn on us. How can they write this shit and get away with it?" he says.

"They're trolls," I say.

"Get your head out of your ass, Clay!"

"I—"

"Someone else wrote, 'I used to work for RASH Airlines as a reserve pilot for five years, and the airline has taken a turn for the worse. We were overworked, and there were times when we skipped checks because management was pressuring us for on-time departures. I won't work for RASH again and I tell my friends to avoid them, too,'" he says. "Tell me who the fuck this *jabrone* asshole pretending to be a pilot is so I can punch him in the face!" Matt says. "You know how I know this comment is fake? Because he calls our checklists *checks*. His nomenclature is off. RASH has never used that tired expression. We use *checklists* every day because that's what they're called. Where's the proof this fucker worked for us? I've been here ten years and never heard management tell us to skip checklists. The hell!" he says.

"Remember the online hostility directed at Monica Lewinsky after her TED talk? The depersonalization from our screens caused people to heap their hatred on her. It's sad, but it's science," I say.

"Save your theories for a term paper. Are you hearing anything I'm saying? This is an avalanche of lies. It's an orchestrated attack!" he says.

The man in the couple next to us seems to be eavesdropping, but I ignore him and put a hand on Matt's shoulder. "It's gonna be OK, man," I say as Matt shakes off my hand.

"Take your fucking hand off me!"

"Give the incident review board a chance to analyze the evidence: statements, logs, interviews, data and voice recorders."

"The kids at my son's school tease him by saying, 'Good evening, ladies and gentlemen from the cockpit. Are you ready to die?' My son asks me why other kids are calling me a loser. What am I supposed to say to my son, Clay? That this is the thanks you get when you save people's lives? Screw your TV news bullshit," Matt says.

"Look, I–"

"Don't pretend you know what you're talking about because you watch *60 Minutes*. I'm *this* close to recommending you for a psych eval, and I *will not* fly with you until you get your shit together," he says.

"I know you're mad and–"

"No shit," Matt says.

"You and Plim are my only friends," I say.

"You're testing the limits of that right now," Matt says.

"I know I'm to blame for what happened, and I'm sorry. Please give the report a chance to set the record straight."

"No one's going to read a 120-page PDF in six months!" he says.

"I'm working on myself and...This city is the loneliest city on earth."

"You fucked up, and I saved everyone, Clay. It's that simple. No one could've taken over in the scenario you handed me—I deserve a parade for what I did, not the shitstorm I'm living in day in and day out. Without me, we would've junked it on Northern Boulevard or in Canarsie with max fatalities."

"I–"

"Get it together, Clay!"

"I know, I mean, I will."

"And get laid. For you, any woman would do at this point...And what was that shit you were jabbering about on the roll?" Matt says.

"I don't–"

"You said 'They're coming.' Who's coming, Clay?" he says.

"I don't know." I toy with my spoon and sigh. "Have you ever thought about him?"

"Who?" Matt says.

"You know, Varsick," I say.

"Sam Varsick?" Matt says. I nod. "You gotta be kidding me. What's your thing with him?" he says.

"Maybe he could help. He's been at RASH forever," I say.

"*Jesus,* Clay. You must be the most gullible person on earth. Sam Varsick is a silverback asshole, and you don't need him in your life. Listen, keep up with this shit and

I'm gonna sick ALPA on your ass, and they'll stuff you on a shrink's couch. *Seriously.* Watch me."

Both of our phones on the table start vibrating with a synchronized pulsing alert.

"The fuck?" Matt says, grabbing his phone and I reach for my phone too.

"The hell is this?"

"RASH Alert Broadcast Notification," Matt says, and now we're both reading our screens. "*Fuck me.* An explosion at the check-in counters at JFK. Twelve dead, forty-three injured and–" Matt says. "There's a message for us. They're–"

"For who? What!?" I say.

"For us. They posted something online and said they're–" Matt says.

"Who? *What the hell!* Lemme see–" I move to get a closer look at his phone.

"They're–"

"Finish your sentence, Matt. They're what?!"

"The bomb only hit the RASH Airlines counter, Clay, and they said they're–"

"*They're what?!*" I yell.

Matt looks up from his phone. "They're coming for us."

5

THE PLATFORM ROSE A DOZEN feet above the audience and was nearly a hundred feet across, but Sumito made use of every inch, prowling its length only to stop occasionally and share a joke with the crowd. The giant stage dwarfed him, but a speaker always looked more impressive when they were presented on a grand scale. A crowd had come to hear the CEO, their numbers rising up around him like spectators at the ancient Colosseum.

"You rarely get what you want at a doctor's appointment," his amplified voice said to the packed house. "You want a skilled doctor who's running on time, but what you get is an interminable wait and seven minutes of care."

The talk's live feed was playing on a screen above the stage, and the video switched between close-ups of Sumito's face and cutaways to audience members rapt with attention.

The fortysomething CEO of Shabba Shabba Technologies looked casual and relaxed in a charcoal gray suit, blue shirt, and brown wingtips from a bespoke London tailor. He wore a wedding band, and a gold watch was visible beyond his shirtsleeve.

"At Shabba Shabba Technologies, we see healthcare differently. Appointments, procedures, and prescriptions should be easy to get." Sumito advanced a slide on his presentation to one that read LET'S GET HEALTHY. "And now they are.

"Introducing the Shabba Shabba app. Now you can order anything for your health using your phone and some biometric inputs. Your request is then reviewed by our virtual healthcare team, and we take immediate action. Ninety-five percent of Shabba Shabba app requests are fulfilled within forty-eight hours. And 99 percent of prescriptions are filled within twenty-four hours."

Sumito paused, anticipating applause, but the theater was silent. He stroked his gray crew cut, smoothed his jacket, and pointed to the screen behind him, which read SAFETY IN THE CLOUD.

"Our triple-encrypted servers store your health information in a secure digital vault with 24/7 protection. We're putting physicians a tap away on your screen because healthcare should bend to your will." Again he paused, hoping for a reaction, but the crowd was quiet. "Order a new prescription from a bus stop, even your kid's boring parent-teacher conference. Kidding! I'm sure your conferences are as entertaining as mine!" He fiddled with his wedding band and waited in silence.

The film crew sensed a problem and hastily ad-libbed applause to fill the void. Meanwhile, the stage director looked around for the sound engineer. The two men finally locked eyes, and the director pantomimed clapping and mouthed, "Add applause and laughter."

The pre-recorded sounds of clapping and laughter boomed throughout the theater too loudly and Sumito jumped. "Bloody hell! What's going on?" he said, looking at the director.

"Sorry, sorry. Sound glitch, Sumito. We'll need a do-over on that last one, mate," Simon, the director, said.

"Great. I'm ready for the do-over," Sumito said.

Simon stared down the sound man and stage whispered: "Not now, Max! Use the fucking cues in the script." He returned to Sumito with a smile. "We'll fix the audio in post. Lovely talk, by the by. Carry on for the do-over!" He returned to the sound man. "Work on your fucking timing, Max!"

The aural sleight of hand was out of sync with the CEO's words, but the sound effects complemented the talk perfectly. The faux adulation made it appear as though an auditorium-sized crowd was riveted by the CEO's words.

Sumito walked to the stage's lip and stood next to a blue 3D logo that read SHABBA SHABBA TECHNOLOGIES. He advanced a slide on his presentation to a screen that read HOME SERVICES.

"Let's move on to home services. Cleaning. Laundry. Grocery shopping. You've got social networking to do! Shabba Shabba Technologies' proprietary service tools let you hire home workers right from your phone. Our workers will clean your home, do your laundry or shopping, and put everything away exactly as you want it. We'll fold your laundry, put it in a wicker basket, and wrap it up with a bow."

Applause filled the theater and Sumito beamed as the overhead video cut to a close-up of his face and then to a two-shot in the crowd. The reaction shot was tight on a pair of thirtysomething women, a blonde and brunette, clapping and smiling. The shorter woman had a blonde bob cut and wore a white blouse and black slacks. She was youthful, with an unfortunate face. The taller brunette had long black hair, a pretty face with high cheekbones like a model, and wore a fashionable white sleeveless business dress with lipstick and heels. She'd put a lot of effort into maximizing the attention paid to her.

Sumito pointed to the screen behind him that read SHABBA SHABBA TECHNOLOGIES. YOU CAN TRUST US.

"We started in 2010, and 'You Can Trust Us' has been our motto from the start. People were skeptical when we launched, but I think history will prove us right. Our vision was to make your life our business, and we've succeeded. Our centralized and secure data warehouses have eliminated the stress of data in the cloud, and our healthcare and home services are only the beginning."

The applause continued as Sumito made his way to the stage's center and fiddled with his watch. Offstage, the director whispered to his assistant: "We'll need more audience reaction shots in post. A seat-filled theater under dim lighting. An affluent crowd wearing those plastic lanyards with names and titles. Caucasians with a few Asians and Indians. No blacks. No Latinos. No fatties. No one over fifty."

"'You Can Trust Us' isn't a catchphrase. It's how we do business," Sumito said. "I use Shabba Shabba employees in my home because they're the most reliable employees on earth. Our employees aren't only licensed and bonded. They're double background checked and have at least ten personal and professional references. They've undergone a battery of personal interviews to check for criminal potential and psychological stability. But you don't have to take my word for it. We have hundreds of online reviews you can read for yourself."

"It sounds like a dream," Petrova whispered to Katrina.

"Or a nightmare." Katrina aimed her plastic smile toward the stage, applauding limply, then brushed back a lock of hair with a manicured hand.

"Bollocks, this wig is hot," Petrova said.

"You'll get used to it."

Sumito walked to stage right and shielded his eyes from the lights as if he were addressing a vast audience.

"Such a great turnout here in New York. We're a British company, and we appreciate the warm welcome we've received in the States. A big thank you to everyone for coming out." He clapped for the audience and applause soon followed, filling the theater.

"We're really proud of what we've built, and a special thank you to the husbands, wives, and partners of our employees who have sacrificed so we could bring you these great services." He brought his palms together and bowed in a *wai*. "Thank you." The theater filled with a long applause break and he sipped from a water bottle.

"You can trust Shabba Shabba Technologies' employees the same way you'd put your trust in, say, an airline pilot when you board a flight...And speaking of flying, we've got something else in store for you, and it's epic."

He clicked his remote to advance to a slide that read LET'S FLY. There was a thunderous applause break with some hoots and hollers, and he held back a smile as he waited for the noise to die down.

"I want to talk about something that everyone has an opinion about: air travel. There's a lot of choice when it comes to flying, but airlines are mostly the same and have the same persistent problems: price gouging, oversold flights, inflated holiday fares, uncomfortable seats, and fees for everything. Sound about right?" The audience hooted. Sumito relished riling them up, teasing what was to come.

"We asked ourselves questions about our own flying experiences. Which airlines were our favorites, and why? What made one airline better than another? And what would it be like to fly on an airline that really cared? One that *loved* taking to the skies?

"As travelers, we were tired of being ripped off. Fees for carry-ons, Wi-Fi, drinks, meals, and luggage. Surcharges for fuel, landing, and security. Ridiculous...Well, we think we've figured out a better way to fly. Would you like to hear about it?"

There was another applause break and Sumito felt himself riding the crest of a wave. He clicked to the next slide and the audience roared even louder. There were hoots and "Yeahs!" and he basked in the seconds-long adulation.

Photographers at the stage's front took pictures, their flashes capturing the image he hoped would lead the day's news. His arms were folded across his chest in the foreground. Behind him, the slide said it all: INTRODUCING SWOOSH AIRLINES.

"Introducing Swoosh Airlines, the first new major international commercial airline in over a decade. We're calling our airline Swoosh because we're bold, efficient, and committed to transforming the way people fly. We have the newest fleet with the most experienced pilots and crew. And unlike other airlines, we didn't buy a bunch of used planes, give them a coat of paint, and slap our logo on the side. We fly brand-new airliners fresh from the factory. Would you like to see one now?"

He pointed at the screen behind him, where a video of a glimmering wide-body jet was soaring through blue skies. The jet's aluminum hull reflected bright sunshine and the livery color scheme was intricate. Sweeping arcs of magenta and gold ran the fuselage's length and met in a shiny infinity symbol next to the words: SWOOSH AIRLINES.

Photographers continued taking photos, and Sumito worked the press like a model, moving his feet, hips, and arms after every flash went off. Laughter filled the audience, and he milked the joke for what it was worth.

"Safety, service, and on-time performance are what we're about. We didn't hire reject pilots from other airlines, either. Ours were hired using our proprietary screening technology to ensure we have the best pilots on earth. And today, we're proud to announce service in seven cities: Atlanta, Dallas, London, Los Angeles, New York, Palm Springs, and Washington D.C. We're going to make things different in air travel, because we love to fly!"

Roaring applause filled the theater and a voice began shouting over the din. The woman's voice grew louder and continued shouting until the clapping died down. Sumito did his best to ignore the heckler and stay on message, but the woman kept at it until it was impossible not to address her.

"Isn't it true that you were a drug addict?!" she yelled out.

"Shit," Petrova whispered from behind her laptop.

"Watch," Katrina said.

"There's some commotion here in the audience," Sumito said. "I wasn't expecting to turn this into a Q&A, but what the heck. Let's give it a shot, shall we? Could you stand up and repeat your question?" he said to the heckler.

The woman stood in silhouette near the stage, her voice loud and clear.

"Is it true that you used to be a drug addict?"

Sumito nodded politely. If he was uncomfortable, he didn't let on.

"Is it OK if I repeat your question so everyone here and watching at home can follow?" He nodded as if hearing her answer, and the woman sat down. "The question was, 'Is it true you used to be a drug addict?'" There were some murmurs in the crowd, but it grew quiet as he walked to the stage's front and bowed his head, then looked above the crowd.

"There's no such thing as privacy in this world of social media and constant connection. I'm a public figure, but I'm also a human being with a family I try to protect so we can live a normal life. I've also tried to keep my private battles *private*. It's true that I've had my struggles..."

"Yes, I was a drug addict for many years, but I've been clean for twenty-six months. I'm a human being and a work in progress, and I have many faults. I think it's important you know about Shabba Shabba Technologies, but please do not focus on my personal battles, for they have nothing to do with our services."

"In fact, I don't think my challenges with addiction are a reason for concern, because millions of people struggle with addiction every day. Addiction is a treatable disease, and our prayers should be with everyone who suffers under its might." Sumito dropped his head to his chest and moved his lips as if saying a prayer.

Roaring applause filled the theater. Sumito waved to someone offstage and blew them a kiss.

"Blimey," Petrova said.

Katrina huffed.

"Any of that true?" Petrova said. Katrina said nothing, just applauded with her same smile.

"Now that this has been sorted, let's move on! Thank you for your question...Shabba Shabba Technologies was born in 2010 with–"

"Isn't it true you're an alcoholic?!"

This voice was louder than the first, coming from a man who stood in the row closest to the stage. People in the audience were talking in low tones, and Sumito used his hands to motion for people to quiet down.

"Sir, I think privacy has a place in every person's life, don't you?" Sumito said. The man yelled out his question louder, but it was clear that it had already been heard by everyone.

"These questions are...a regrettable turn of events on this happy day of company announcements. I have no desire to share the details of my whole life on this stage because my wife and young son are here today, and besides, these are personal matters." He gestured offstage to an unseen family and mouthed, "I'm sorry."

"In the name of transparency, I'll repeat this question as well...The questioner asked if I struggle with alcohol addiction. The answer is, *No, I don't*. However, I did in the past. I'm a recovering alcoholic and proud of it. I've been sober for over ten years...Now, Shabba Shabba was born in 2010 with a mission of bringing...I'm...I'm sorry...Please...I need a moment."

He turned away from the cameras with his head bowed and hands at his sides as if he'd been overcome with emotion. It was the first break in the talk's flow and it seemed the wind had left his sails. He took a breath and turned back around.

"The Shabba Shabba app is platform agnostic and portable, phone, tablet, laptop, watch, PC. And please, come fly Swoosh Airlines." And with that, he turned and walked offstage without so much as a goodbye. The sound of applause filled the theater, and then it was silent.

"And...we're clear!" the director called out.

Sumito marched back onstage full of energy. "That, my friends, is the power of empathy," he said, bowing to the camera. "Now get this thing off me." He struggled to remove his lavalier microphone from his lapel. "It's like a morgue in here and hot as balls. Do we have any water? And let's have a decent lunch for once. Place an order for everyone and use my credit card!" The sound man approached him, but not before Sumito ripped the mic from his lapel and yanked off the battery pack, dumping them into the man's hands.

He walked over to the director and clapped a hand on his shoulder. "How'd we do, Simon?"

"I was feeling sorry for you myself, you old codger!" Simon said. The director sat in a folding chair, leaning back so that it was propped up on two legs against the wall. "This'll play well to people's emotions. They'll want you to succeed. Very, very good," he said.

Sumito smiled and massaged the director's shoulders.

"Impossible without you, Simon. Cheers!"

There was a vast open space in front of the men where the crowd should've been, but the "audience" was composed of Katrina, Petrova, and a dozen extras hired for the occasion. Camera angles had been created to make it appear as though a vast audience were present even though the production occupied a small corner of a midtown soundstage. There was no amphitheater, no crowd, and no press in sight.

"Let's edit this right away and get it online. I'll grab the girls," Sumito said.

"This will give a huge bump to your '*Q*' score, especially for Swoosh Airlines," Simon said. The director crossed his arms over his chest as a dialog box popped up on his screen. His expression changed and now he was clicking on the screen and typing commands in the terminal window.

"Tits," Sumito said, smiling broadly. "Cheers, mate."

"Fuck...There's been a bit of a recording problem. Our hard disk array failed," Simon said.

"OK. Again, punter, but this time without the nerd talk," Sumito said.

"Our hard disk...the recording server...the recording is gone."

"We have to re-shoot?!" Sumito said.

"Not all of it, but we'll need a do-over on the last fifteen minutes."

"*Shit!*" Sumito began pacing back and forth by the fire exit, grinding his teeth as Simon turned his laptop around to show his boss. The screen showed they'd only captured the talk's first minute.

"I'm sorry, mate. We'll need a do-over. We can stay until it's finished," Simon said.

"*You can stay until it's finished!?* I know *you'll* stay until it's finished!" Sumito's leg jutted out and caught Simon's chair, kicking it out from under him. The director toppled over and his laptop followed, cracking its screen.

"Great. I'm ready for the do-over." Sumito said.

6

THIRTY-SECOND STREET IS THE SECOND worst place in Manhattan, but I don't say that with any malice toward midtown. I'm just telling the truth about a place New Yorkers hate.

Manhattan's belt loop is a part of the city you try to avoid, like Times Square, because it embodies a certain kind of city angst: tight sidewalks with no breathing space. The only people who come here on purpose have a quick to-do. Those who arrive by accident have to divine their way out.

You could call 32nd Street a hub if you were feeling generous—Macys, the Empire State Building, and Koreatown are here—but even these charms haven't increased its appeal. Every time I emerge here from the train, I feel like a whale breaking the surface, counting the seconds until I can return to the comfort of the deep.

But Sam Varsick loves it here, and he makes this point to me over text as we finalize our plans to meet up. But now, as my train nears Herald Square, I wonder what I hope to gain from meeting the man HazMatt dislikes so vehemently.

My quads burn as I climb the steps onto Broadway and am met with a curtain of heat. I don my sunglasses, then wend my way east on 32nd toward the meeting spot.

There's a tall, older Caucasian man in the distance a half-block away looking out with sunglasses on. He looks out of place in the predominantly Korean neighborhood because, well...he's a tall white guy in a Korean neighborhood. But the gray-haired man is situationally aware and scanning all sectors of approach like a Secret Service agent. I note his firm, upright posture and air of authority, and realize he's got a bead on me, too.

We acknowledge each other like a couple of jungle cats, evaluating our gaits for strength and speed. *I could take him*, I think, but the tightness in my chest is real, and the discomfort grows stronger as we approach the intersection.

"You're Matt Blancando's left-hand seat," Sam says.

"HazMatt? Matt? Yeah. He's my F.O. Good kid."

"Let's get off the street...this way," Sam says, walking past me in the direction I came from. He's wearing a pair of crisp khakis, a polo shirt, and a gold watch jangles from his wrist. "This fucking heat. My ball sack is stuck to my leg and I can't shake it loose."

He looks like a retired game show host from the side—tan, leathery, affluent—with a face lined with wrinkles and a yellowing moustache. I'm guessing he's in his sixties and has been smoking since before there was Internet.

There's a puff of smoke as he exhales. "God *damn*, look at all this young ass," he says, eyeing some student bodies.

His cigarette is flicked to the street and hits a parked car, sparking like a firework.

He definitely looks like a silverback captain, with the helmet of silver hair, paunch, and orange glow. I'm guessing he's back from sunny climes—or a spray tan booth—but he seems happy enough in this neighborhood, if a bit out of place.

"The train stations are hotter than hell in summer and cold as a fuck in winter. We ride the same system from when Teddy Roosevelt was president, but suffer more indignities. There were no hoods announcing 'It's show time!' back then. No fake homeless workers tried to shake you down for a dollar. No buskers banging on buckets or bongos. The trains have ruined drumming for me, man. I hate drums," he says.

"Nice to meet you, by the way. I'm Clay."

"When I retire, it's good riddance New York. I'm gonna hop a bird to a galaxy far, far away. Ko Samui. The Seychelles. Avignon. Southern Japan. Anywhere the beer is cold and flip-flops are considered footwear. One-way, motherfucker." He points across the street. "This way."

"I'm not sure if I'm up for a massage."

"Let's get our joints worked on," he says.

Sam grabs his nether region and shifts the contents until a smile spreads across his face. "Christ, that that feels better. We go through the bodega with the lottery signs and we're in." He accelerates past some slow walkers and I hurry to keep up, like a Hollywood assistant.

"You go on ahead. I wanted to ask you about my job and—"

"Greeks, Turks, Japanese. They all get massages together, not like us uptight Americans," he says.

"I'm not a spa guy. Nothing personal. How do I get my job—"

"Relax, Clay. I'm not going to stare at your junk." Sam steps into the street, crossing mid-block, and I follow behind.

A bicyclist barrels down on me ringing his bell, going against traffic. "Yo! Yo! *Yo!*" he yells as I pivot out of the way a second before I'm side-swiped.

"Immigrant fucker," Sam says.

"I'll see how I feel once we get there," I say.

Second-floor signs above the street advertise SPA and MASSAGE services with neon arrows pointing to the downstairs entrances. A few staircases we pass have placards for shiatsu and Swedish treatments depicting women's hands on male bodies in Photoshopped paradises. One place we pass has a sign out front that says simply: LET US RELAX YOU SPA.

"Wish we could machine gun those fuckers who bombed the terminal," he says.

"That ain't the half of what I want to do. The security briefing was shit," I say.

"The usual, 'If you see something, say something,'" Sam says.

"How do I do it?"

"It's a *massage*, man. The girls take us to separate rooms for a shower and we come back and they rub us down. Don't flatter yourself. I don't want to suck your cock," he says.

"*No!*" I say. "How do I get my job back?"

"I wish they were as good at flying as they were at massage," he says.

"What? Who's they?"

"*Them,*" Sam says, nodding to the people around us on 32nd Street.

He peels left off the sidewalk into a cramped bodega, tight with newspapers, snacks, and refrigerators humming with drinks. The owner eyes us suspiciously until he recognizes Sam and a smile lights his face.

"*Orenmanida!*" the bodega owner says, clapping his hands together.

"I know. I know. *Annyeong hashimnikka! Joeun haru dweseyo!*" Sam says.

The owner bows, then points at the ceiling with a finger. "*Joeun haru dweseyo!*"

"Second floor, Clay," Sam says.

"I'll hang back while you go in."

We climb a rusting staircase and arrive at a landing with a yellow sign written in Korean hanging on a metal door. There's a single buzzer and a few postcards tacked to its front showing a handsome man lying on a massage table near a waterfall with lots of pink flowers.

The door buzzer is pressed and there's the sound of footsteps inside the suite. "*Anyoung hashimnikka!*" says a muffled chorus of female voices as a metal latch is turned. The door cracks open and a set of female eyes look us over.

"Sam!" a voice says as the door swings open to reveal two smiling women with long dark hair. The thirtysomething women wear robes and smiles and have their hands at their sides. The taller woman rushes to Sam and puts her arms around his neck, kissing him on the cheek.

"Girls, this is Clay. Clay, this is Sook-Joo and Bong-Cha." He points from the shorter woman to the taller one. "Shit, maybe it's the other way around!" He laughs. He wraps his arms around Bong-Cha and kisses her, his raspy laugh filling the air. "I think I got that right, they all look the same!"

"Come on. That's racist," I say.

Sook-Joo smiles at me and bows. "*Mannaseo bangapseumnida.* I'm Sook."

"Clay. *Mannaseo bangapseumnida.*" I bow in return.

"Let's get out of this fucking heat, bro. You want a half hour or an hour?"

Sook leads me inside the suite and takes the backpack off my shoulders. My hand is now in hers and she leads me down the hallway away from Sam.

"See you in awhile, tiger!" he says.

"Wait! What were you talking about earlier?" I turn to face him down the passageway and find he and Bong-Cha arm-in-arm by the front door.

"Don't be a pussy, Clay. Get over yourself and admit it."

"Admit what? I don't understand." I take my hand from Sook and head back to him. An air conditioner hums in the hallway while the women pull items from a nearby shelf.

"Do you want to get real, or do you want an 'A' in Ethnic Studies? Get over your white guilt, Clay."

"I'm biracial, Sam. Half-white, half-Korean. There's no white guilt here."

"I'm talking about *them*. They're always asking for permission and deferring to authority. That shit doesn't work in the cockpit," he says.

I stare at him.

"I'm talking about the *Asian problem*," Sam says. The women are now at our sides holding folded robes and silk slippers.

"I don't like where this is going. Not at all. I'm sure I'm going to regret asking, but what *Asian problem*? I'm here to find out how to get my job back," I say.

Bong-Cha pulls on Sam's arm to lead him away, but he stands his ground, kissing her shoulder and caressing her arm. "Just a minute, baby," he says, then looks at me. "One word, bro: Rio."

"The crash last year?" I say. "What does that have to do with anything? It was a tragic accident."

"Late morning. Bright sunshine. Five mile per hour winds and twenty miles of visibility in every direction. You coulda taken a piss on the runway without your stream blowing on your pant leg. And the crew *still* fucked the landing. A miracle that more people weren't killed," Sam says.

"It was an accident," I say.

"No wind shear. No wake turbulence. No software problems. No mechanical problems. No ATC or tech issues and not a cloud in the fucking sky. How do you kill ten people, injure 96, and destroy a $120 million dollar airliner in conditions like that?" Sam slides a hand down Bong-Cha's body and rests his fingers on the small of her back. "I'll tell you how you fuck up a landing like that...By being Asian."

"Shit, Sam. You're such a racist!" I say.

"*I'm the racist!?* You ever hear of the ethnic theory of plane crashes? An over-deference to authority is toxic in the cockpit. Some cultures defer to seniority too much and that's bad for air safety, but I'm the racist, right, so case closed? You can sleep well tonight, except the problem isn't solved, and passengers are in danger. And now you're going to lecture me because *you're* Asian."

"No, I'm going to lecture you because I'm a human being. You can't generalize an entire culture," I say.

"Why not? Even if it's true? To you, the truth isn't as important as being politically correct," he says.

"Some Asian carriers were involved in fatal accidents decades ago, but the problem was fixed. Take a look at the big Asian airlines and you'll find phenomenal safety records," I say.

"Four stripes doesn't make you the cockpit's overlord, Clay. I expect my F.O. to be my right-hand when we fire up the turbines. The first officer's job is to speak up if there's a concern, even if there's going to be disagreement. Aren't you curious what they did that miraculously fixed those ethnic cockpit problems?"

"This is tired old news. The problem was fixed and everyone knows it."

"Then what really happened in Rio?" Sam says.

"'Mismanaged descent rate,' is what the investigators cited," I say.

"Then why the spate of recent Asian crashes? I've noticed a new trend of Asian carrier problems and I'm not allowed to bring it up? You can only learn when you bring the facts to light, Clay. It's not racist to talk about ethnic differences if they have to do with air safety. The psychology of the cockpit is just as important as maintenance or air traffic, but no one wants to talk about it."

"This is a safe space, Sam. What's your point?"

"My point is alarm bells should go off when a commercial jet crashes without an obvious mechanical problem. Last year, that other Asian carrier flew into an embankment on approach in Portugal. They hit a sea wall in broad daylight and sheared the landing gear off. The plane spun around and burst into flames, killing seven and injuring twenty-four. My grandmother could land a commercial jet on a freeway off ramp in conditions like that."

"So, an Asian carrier crashed? So have all global carriers. The Rio crash investigators cited an overreliance on automation," I say.

"What does that mean?" he says. "Sounds like a senior captain set the computer for the wrong ILS approach and the first officer was too timid to speak up. Computers only do what we program them to do."

Sook-Joo answers a ringing telephone and Bong-Cha says something to her in Korean. The women converse back and forth, conveying information to the caller on the phone. A truck barrels down 32nd Street, grinding its gears loudly, and reminds me we're smack-dab in midtown.

"A plane using automation is like a car on cruise control, Clay. If it's doing something you don't like, you grab the controls and take over. If your glide path is off and you're coming in too low and slow, someone should speak up. A culture that doesn't encourage you to question authority is going to have a fucked up group of pilots. The studies have proven it: unchallenged authority in the cockpit is unsafe."

"Correlation isn't causation, Sam. You're painting all Asian carriers as bad based on isolated incidents."

"No. I'd fly with anyone in my right-hand seat if they were born in the US or Europe."

"So, all non-Western pilots are bad? Everyone in the Middle East? Africa? China, Japan, Korea, Southeast Asia, Turkey, India, and Russia. The lot of them?" I say.

"Wrong-o again, Clay. I'm not talking about competence. I'm talking about a cultural problem where first officers are putting their captains on pedestals. This makes F.O.s fearful of speaking up because they think disagreement is disrespect. The result is a cockpit dictatorship with unchallenged authority, and that's unsafe. I'm not saying all non-Western pilots are incompetent. I'm saying they're not taught to be assertive before things go tits up," Sam says.

"These are the same tired clichés. Asian men are meek, spineless, feminine," I say.

"I grew up playing with Lionel trains, Legos, and Hot Wheels while these guys were playing video games and eating fermented cabbage. Who would you rather have at the controls?"

"Shit. You really are an asshole, Sam."

"Maybe I am. I'm out of touch with the young people, but that doesn't mean I'm wrong." He slides a hand down Bong-Cha's body and takes the robe and slippers from her. "I'm going to relax, and you should too. In fact, enjoy yourself here as long as you want. My treat. They have my credit card on file, so you can enjoy a spa day. Relax. You need it."

Sam takes Bong-Cha's hand and leads her down the hallway toward the shower room. She bows to him in front of the showers and starts removing his shoes. The shower room door opens to a hiss of steam and a cloud of vapor.

"Hey! Just so you know, the Asian carrier in Rio did what they were supposed to! They used the plane's automation coupled to an instrument landing system approach!" I say. Sam pushes the shower door closed without entering and looks at me.

"An instrument landing system wasn't designed for regular visual approaches, Clay. It was made SOP by nervous nelly airline administrators who didn't think their pilots could get their fucking planes on the field. Cat III ILS is the most challenging landing scenario. It requires rock-solid training and trust in the computers on the plane and on the ground. It was designed for blowing snow white outs when you can't see your dick in your hand. It's for when sheets of rain are buffeting the cockpit and wind is maxing out the controls. It's for fog and zero visibility and when you've only got one shot to get the fucking bird on the field. Landing a plane without an ILS isn't an accomplishment, Clay. It's a Tuesday."

"I want to get reinstated. I want my job back at RASH. What should I do?" I say.

"Look at the last ten fatal crashes. Three out of ten were Asian airlines. What does that tell you?" Sam says.

"It tells me the majority *weren't* Asian airlines," I say.

"So I'm supposed to give the Asian Rio pilots credit for using automation when they *still* killed people? Ever try landing an airplane in broad daylight without a computer? I'd like to introduce you to Wilbur and Orville Wright."

"I think you're being a little harsh...How do I get back into RASH and–"

"Here's how you land an airliner. You line up the runway in your windshield and land the plane on the center line. And hearing the Rio pilots on the voice recordings makes me sick...yakking about their shitty 401(k) plans. Fuck them."

"What should I do now?"

"Honor your carrier. That's the bottom line. You don't dedicate your life to an airline and talk shit about them. You build something with them because they've invested in you...The only people I have sympathy for in the Rio crash are the passengers and crew. The pilots deserve to fry for being such assholes."

"Yeah, but–"

"And I'm sorry you got doxed, man," Sam says.

"What?"

"On the hidden Internet. It's some Wild West shit on there. Sorry, bro."

I stare at him.

"Doxed. It means someone leaked your personal info on the Dark Web to embarrass you. They posted your home address, telephone number, Amazon purchase history, employers, salary. That's some fucked up shit right there."

"*Shit.* Who do you think did it? And–"

"Jesus, Clay," Sam sighs. "You need to man up and start thinking for yourself. Do something. Our carrier is under attack and all you care about is your job? I'm tired of arguing. Besides, I've got to get up early tomorrow, and I need to relax."

Sam nods to Bong-Cha, and she opens the shower room door to a cloud of vapor that fills the hallway. She smiles at him, takes his hand, and then they step inside, vanishing into the mist.

7

The man in seat 33E screamed, and Jill
Parabola looked up in time to see a college
girl finish him off with an elbow to the
head. The man crumpled onto his tray table
with a knife in his temple and blood on his
clothing. The college girl sneered at the
dead man's bloody suit.

"That's gonna need a good dry cleaning,"
she said, then looked at her watch.

The passengers in economy were now
screaming, but US Air Marshal Jill Parabola
had trained for scenarios like this and was
incognito on the Athens-bound flight. Jill
wasn't about to intervene—not yet—she would
wait to ensure there were no sleepers
onboard who could get the jump on her if
she made a move.

Federal Air Marshal Jill Parabola's mind
was already working, and she envisioned
what was next for the lumbering airliner,
reasoning the terrorists would take control
in short order. The terrorists could re-
route them to another country or turn them
into a missile to strike any target at
will. If only Jill had been more aware
during boarding. If only she'd noticed the
blonde college girl's behavior before she
struck. But the time for wishful thinking
was over: The attack was underway.

A man stood and surprised the college girl
with a semi-automatic at point-blank range.
The gun's muzzle was jammed into her ribs
and the two locked eyes before a bang rang
out to more screams. The man dropped his
gun to his side without a word, then looked
at the college girl in disbelief as blood
bloomed on his shirt like a flower before
he fell back into his seat, dead.

"Please do remain seated," a fat man in an
adjacent row said to the man he'd just
killed. The fat hijacker holstered his
smoking gun, wiped the sweat from his face,
and looked to the girl. He was panicking
and pointing at his watch.

The first class curtain swept open and a
middle-aged man in a gray suit sauntered
down the aisle carrying champagne and two
glasses. The terrorists stepped aside at
the sight of their leader, who smiled at

them before looking at the two FBI agents who lay dead in their seats.

"Sir, I'm very sorry! The FBI is taken care of, but we're two minutes behind schedule," the plump and sweaty terrorist said to the boss. The leader removed a handgun from a dead FBI agent and pointed it at the fat man's head. "Please, sir! I'm very sorry. Very, very sorry. Please accept my apology!" the fat man stammered to his boss.

A shot rang out and blood spurted from the fat man's head as he collapsed to the floor.

"Apology accepted," the leader said, then looked to the college girl.

Go and kill a few people, then go to the cockpit and ask to be let in. Whatever you do, don't kill any flight attendants— someone has to serve drinks." The man then turned to speak to the ambassador seated between the two dead FBI agents.

"Good evening, Ambassador," the leader said in a British accent. "I hope you're having a lovely flight. Listen, I'd love it if you'd accompany me up front for a drink. It would give us a chance to..." He caressed the ambassador's cheek with a finger and she recoiled "...get better acquainted."

"The US government doesn't negotiate with terrorists!" the ambassador glared.

"Ah, Madam Ambassador, I believe you misunderstand your predicament. We didn't come here for your government." And then he paused. *"We came for you."*

A THUNDER CLAP BOOMS THROUGH my home theater and the TV cuts to black as the theme music kicks in and the credits roll. Another episode is over, so I stretch and yawn, flipping my body around on the couch to find a more comfortable position.

There's a ton of paperwork on the bookshelves and desk of my studio apartment, reminding me that I have a lot to get done today. I sigh at the clutter and already feel overwhelmed even though I haven't touched the piles. It's hard getting motivated when I'm downroute—not flying—and I'm bored of eating Raisin Bran and masturbating.

Jill Parabola, US Air Marshal is my latest TV indulgence. The show wows me because it's got great drama. The plots are realistic, and I get steeped in the fictional world of aviation law enforcement. I've even become a series' fanboy, hanging out on the show's online forums so I can discuss the latest plot twists.

Most of the nights I'm home, I'll download an episode so I can watch Jill Parabola protect the skies over the United States and kick terrorist ass. I didn't think I'd fall so helplessly for Jill's character, a middle-aged divorcée and single mom who loves handguns and chocolate-sprinkle cupcakes, but I have. I'll even search out the show's New York City locales so I can take photos in front of them and brag online.

There's a buzz from my phone on the couch with a text from HazMatt reminding me of a memorial service for the airport bombing victims. The recovery effort at the international terminal is still underway, and victims are being identified, which means more stories will keep New Yorkers in their well of grief.

There's a lot of patriotic flag waving going on as the FBI and NYPD search for the attackers. New York City may be in mourning, but TV and social media are rife with angry protests calling for revenge in the attack's wake. This was the first domestic terror event since September 11, and many people want our nation to take swift military action on the world stage.

Two RASH employees were killed in the attack, and three are listed as missing, and it makes my blood boil. My work family was attacked and on our home soil no less, so nothing can be the same again. No one I personally knew was a victim, but that's cold comfort considering the close-knit bond we share. *When something happens to one of us, it happens to all of us.* RASH has always been like family, so we're all in shock and grief. Meanwhile, relatives and friends of the missing wait for news outside International Departures Terminal C as rescuers comb the debris for survivors.

Over the weekend, I swung by RASH Operations to get some things from my locker, but only realized the stupidity of my undertaking once I was en route. There was the hellacious traffic and then the two-plus hours of waiting at security checkpoints with my RASH ID and passport. But once I got there, I was surprised to find our second floor offices intact.

A tiny video camera was still high on the wall in the hallway where I'd placed it a month before, dutifully recording in silence. I plucked the silvery device off the wall with a high jump and stuffed it in my pocket. I don't think anyone was the wiser.

Part of me was afraid that the anger over the attacks and the cries of "U-S-A! U-S-A!" in the streets would force the government to unleash Predator drone strikes on some unsuspecting hamlet. The last thing I'd want is for an innocent group to be on the receiving end of a Hellfire missile before we know what's what. A more sensible approach would be...would be...*What do I care about sensible?!* I wanted to get these fuckers and give them what they deserve!

The public wants action, not words, although the government's stance is presently more "dove" than "hawk." That's good news because it means it's unlikely the administration will go off half-cocked on some presumed target. I don't agree with the executive branch's passive stance on terror, but at least we're not going to send a missile down someone's chimney.

Meanwhile, RASH brass is asking us to go about our duties like it's business as usual. *Yes, RASH Airlines was attacked, but leave the rest to law enforcement.* That's what we're hearing, but it's an odd directive since the majority of us are military veterans. We're used to answering violence with violence—it's our military creed—because we're warriors first and pilots second. And right now, we're in complete agreement about how to answer this slaughter.

Our bloodlust may be strong, but we have to temper our desires while RASH management reaches out daily with calls for patience. And to those requests I say we will be calm—until we find those fuckers, and then it's gloves off. And yet I have to be careful because my job is in the balance and I must abide by the rules if I want that job back—and I do.

I rise from the couch and move to my kitchen table, where I extract the memory cards from the video cameras. These are the motion-sensing cameras I set up in the cockpit and terminal to capture RASH operations for a short film I wanted to make. I nearly forgot that the cameras had been collecting video on the sly for so long, but all I need now is some interesting footage so I can put together a small film to satisfy my creative jonesing.

The computer chimes as it boots up and I insert the memory cards, dragging the files to my desktop. Maybe Matt's right in calling my video hobby weird, but the cameras capture great quality footage with a documentary feel.

I've always been an amateur storyteller, and maybe I can prepare for a retirement career in digital video by honing my chops in the coming decades. Who knows? I could find myself with a small online fan club and get some reviews and upvotes on my work.

The phone buzzes with another text from Matt. The message includes a video link followed by a bunch of frowny emojis. I open the link on my computer to see what Matt's upset about and lean back to watch the video play in full screen.

The CEO of a British company is making an announcement at a New York City press conference with a packed house. I fast-forward and find the CEO, Sumito Goldberg, announcing the company's plans to expand into commercial air travel.

The company, Swoosh Airlines, will start service immediately with routes in many of RASH Airlines' hubs. The airline has newer planes and cheaper fares and is operating in several key markets—they're going to eat our lunch if we're not careful.

I watch the video for a few minutes and see some women in the audience applauding, including a spectacular beauty with long hair, tan skin, red lips, and...*she's a brunette with long straight hair.* She smiles as the camera zooms in on her—definitely a cutie. I watch a few more seconds of the video, then move on to my editing.

I advance through the first long clip using the "scrubber" tool to get through the boring parts and arrive at video of Matt and me as sunshine paints the cockpit. It's hard to know exactly where we're flying without turning on the audio, but I mouse through the hours-long clip to discover nothing of interest.

My attention flags after twenty minutes, and I realize I'm going to need to automate to speed things up—a software batch process seems like the best idea. The software can automatically analyze each video and pull "selects" to reduce my fatigue.

I set the parameters for the software to locate clips with "rapid motion" and "facial close-ups" so I can hone in on footage that's more interesting. I also want footage from before the airport attack, so I set the date field to sort the results accordingly. I click START, then stand up and stretch my legs.

Standing by the windowsill, I'm happy to find my house plants are on their way back to health after months of neglect. I repotted them, and the bigger pots and fertilizer seem to have done wonders for their growth. The snake plant's leaves jut up to the ceiling like swords, and my Boston fern has lots of fluffy new growth. I return to my computer where thumbnails are growing on my screen like a collage.

I must have hundreds of hours of footage from the recordings, and the software goes to work devouring the video like a hungry man at an all-you-can-eat buffet. The software is analyzing the video and sending still images to my screen, rapid fire.

The first stills feature Matt making silly faces at the camera, hamming it up with frowns and smiles, but they're soon overlapped by images from the terminal camera. People are walking in the corridor outside RASH's operations center hours before the attack. They tile my screen like a mosaic.

A beautiful blonde appears onscreen, and I pause the batch process so I can watch a video of her outside the operations center. She's on the younger side with a phone in her hand and no luggage—late twenties, maybe. She has long blonde hair that falls past her shoulders and is wearing jeans and a tank top. She must be lost, I think, and she finally turns around and walks out of frame. Just another New York City beauty. *Next clip. Restart batch.*

My phone buzzes with a text from Sam Varsick that includes a link to the hidden Internet "doxing" campaign done on me. This was the hack he'd told me about that took a lot of my private information and dumped it online without my consent in an effort to embarrass or humiliate me.

Using the so-called "Dark Web" or hidden Internet like this strikes me as cowardly, but apparently someone's interested enough that they've gone ahead and done the deed. I don't really care what's online, reasoning I've made my mistakes and I can live with them. Besides, who's to say the "information" they've posted is even authentic?

The Dark Web gets my respect for its anonymity, privacy, and protection of political dissidents, but using it like this is pathetic. Its anonymity is a double-edged sword that both protects civil liberties and also enables scofflaws to operate with impunity. There's a link to the site in Sam's text, but it's only accessible with a special web browser, and I don't have time for it now.

A couple of travelers wander down the hallway with roller suitcases in tow, looking lost. I pause the batch and watch as someone kindly approaches them and points them back to international departures. There are lots of head nods and smiles as they walk out of frame. *Next clip. Restart batch.*

A RASH pilot in uniform walks the mezzanine corridor toting a roller bag. Watching him walk the hallway reminds me of how we all use body language to convey our feelings and desires. We show our confidence or insecurities, anger or joy, in how we walk or hold our heads. I think I'd make a good body language expert because I notice how people move and where they put their hands and arms. *Next clip. Restart batch.*

Another pretty woman walks down the hallway, but this one's a little older, probably mid-thirties, wearing a corduroy skirt, heels, with thick straight dark hair. *A brunette with long hair.* There's no question she hit the genetic jackpot, so I play the video to watch her traverse the mezzanine, and my pulse quickens.

I stand up to get something to drink and discover a few wrinkled uniform jackets in a pile on my couch. They remind me I've got some dry cleaning to do and that I'll be back in the cockpit this coming Monday. I can't wait. A simulator checkride is the only thing between me and the skies, and the evaluation is essentially a rubber stamp before I return to active duty.

I return to the attractive brunette's clip and watch her sashay down the hallway with her shopping bags. She's got a pretty face with full lips shaped like Cupid's bow. She passes the RASH offices swinging her hips like a model— she really knows how to work it.

She walks past RASH's operations center, then turns around and walks back into frame and stares inside the offices from a distance. She's staring through the glass like a Peeping Tom, then pivots around abruptly and walks off screen. I rewind the clip, take a screen grab of her face, and send it to my phone. But there's something about her that's curious, so I enlarge her image on the screen.

I bring up the Swoosh Airlines announcement video on my other monitor and stop it on the audience reaction shot with the attractive brunette. Now I have *two* brunettes on my computer monitors, and I enlarge the announcement video and the terminal camera footage so I can compare the images side by side. *Shit.* It's the same woman.

8

SCUZZBUCKET SCRATCHES HIS FACE AND kills the lights on the truck, and now you're both freezing in the dark, his tailgate illuminated by the parking lights of your rental car. He leans against the truck's tailgate with a foot cocked on the bumper, and he eyes you shifting back and forth trying to get warm. The desert dirt crunches underfoot as you stamp your feet then look at your watch, which reads 4:32 A.M.

The hatch of the dust-caked Durango pops open and Scuzzbucket eyes your hands.

"Take your hands out of your pockets. I didn't catch your, uh–" There's menace in his eyes as a vapor cloud escapes his mouth.

"Dave."

"Dave, huh? Well listen here, *Dave*, show me your fucking hands."

"Here you go. We're good."

Now that your hands are at your sides, you realize the knife you brought for self-defense is useless, out of play on account of the fact that you couldn't get to it if you needed to. *You stupid amateur.* You're standing there freezing your ass off and are hit with the realization that you're unfit for life's underbelly. *Dave? What kind of made-up name is that?* Scuzzbucket could easily carve you up like a piece of scrimshaw and toss you in the desert scrub.

"A nine with an eight-shot mag will solve your problem, and if it don't, you're in the wrong business."

"Sorry?"

"Think small, Dave. You need something small that fits in your hands. Forget your fantasies of being a badass, because Glocks and .44 mags weren't made for people like you." A snarl is on his lips and he eyes you with contempt.

Headlights smear the darkness as cars whip by on Twentynine Palms Boulevard and you contemplate your next moves. *Buy a gun. Don't get killed. And make it home alive.* You squeeze your fists in an effort to keep the blood moving in your hands while trading halos of breath by the roadside. The Morongo Valley stars overhead look fake, like an observatory planetarium.

"You're a big man with big hands. What's your business, Dave?"

"Traveling salesman."

"I respect that. I'm a gettin' around man myself, but I love the desert for the crispy chicken." Scuzzbucket laughs as headlights sweep through a nearby parking lot, then stiffens and tracks the car until it's out of sight.

The wind is knocked out of you and you're thrust against the hood, hands roaming your torso and legs. You're spread eagle with a cheek frozen against the steel, trying to remain calm. There's a squeeze on your cock as he checks you for weapons, then a chummy thump on the back. *Shit. I can't believe he didn't he find the knife.*

"I hope you didn't bring company, *Dave*. I trust Mario from the airport, and he says you're a cool dude, but don't fuck with me."

"We're good."

The canvas bag in the truck's hatch looks like a woman's tote. It clatters as it rakes across the carpeted floor. Scuzzbucket dons a pair of gloves and reaches in with one hand.

"You want balance, a good feel in your hands. That's what you need," he says as vapor puffs from his nostrils.

"Sure."

His lips tighten as he presents you with a small semi-auto with burnishing on the barrel and stock and nicks on the muzzle. The brassing has removed some of the 9 mm pistol's finish.

"It's used?"

"It's *loved*, Dave. But trust me, no one's going to miss her. Still, I wouldn't go an' register her serial number at your local PD. Know what I'm sayin'?"

"Feels OK."

"Feels more than OK, *Dave*. She's got eight in the mag and one in the snout, and that gives you power and control. You've got large hands, so you can move her around easy, like a spinner." His coarse laugh is in the air and a hand slaps your back.

A small breeze chills you as you point the gun in the truck's trunk and squeeze the trigger. There's a satisfying click as the metal hammer snaps against the chamber.

"The fuck you doing!?"

Scuzzbucket grabs the pistol and points it at the sky as the magazine drops into his palm. The slide is racked and breech inspected before the magazine is slapped into the butt, slide closed, and safety engaged.

"*Christ.* Fucking amateur night."

The pistol is back with you and you point it at the ground, flicking off the safety. You squeeze the trigger quickly, hammer clicking in a steady rhythm like a factory conveyor belt.

"Bam! Bam! Bam! Them fuckers dead for sure!" His coarse laughter is in the air again.

The chicken burgers across the highway are supposed to be good, crispy patties slathered in barbecue sauce and mayo—the best in Yucca Valley, says the dude at the BP station. But there'll be little time to dawdle after your purchase, 'cause you're due at LAX later this morning. Maybe you'll dine behind the wheel with Steely Dan on the radio, the heater on full blast, and your new purchase at your side.

"Cheap semi-autos are nothin' but bar whores, good for a few minutes but useless long term. They'll give you comfort, then burn your dick when you least expect it. What you want her for?"

"I've never had an enemy before, but I now I do. It's time I had a gun."

"I like your thinkin'. Now a lot of guys want adjustable sights, but you don't need 'em. It's not like you're doin' target practice at a hundred yards."

Scuzzbucket takes the pistol and points it at the highway, tracking headlights as they zoom through the darkness. He sets his sights on a minivan and follows it as it races by like a cheetah. *Click.*

"Bam!" He laughs loudly.

"I'll take her. I had a semi-auto in my twenties...and I need bullets."

"4.4 lb. trigger pull for single action. 26.5 ounces. 6.5 inches long. Light as fuck."

"You got ammunition?"

"Silver tips. Hollow points. Radioactive tracers. Pig-heads. Prebs."

"Something with stopping power," you say.

"I recommend pig-heads because duds are less likely. I'll throw in fifty and the primers are new. I'll do you for $350 out the door plus some FBs to add some bang to your day." Scuzzbucket points the gun at the sky and inhales deeply, taking in the sweeping panorama of stars.

"FBs?"

"Wanna know the biggest scare in the world?" he says, vapor puffing from his mouth.

A lightning bolt strikes the ground and oxygen is sucked from your lungs like a punch to your gut. You're leveled flat, squirming in the dirt, struggling for air with ears screaming in pain. Scuzzbucket looms over you with the pistol in his waistband and fingers in his ears. His mouth is moving in an expression that looks like laughter but there's no sound coming from his lips.

"*Pbler fgal? Asdfha msn? Sonrm deknl?*" he says. The unintelligible gibberish sounds like a whisper from a mile away.

A high-pitched squeal is ringing in your ears as he yanks you to your feet by the scruff of your jacket. His mouth continues moving until the sounds resolve into words.

"You OK?" he says, laughing. "I'll throw in a few at no extra charge. They'll scare the shit out of–"

"The fuck was that?" you say, wiping dirt from your ass with equilibrium sloshing in your head.

"SWAT-grade flashbangs. Harmless concussive grenades. I've got hundreds of them. I'll give you a few with your $350 purchase."

"$350? But Mario said $150." You're swaying like a drunk and trying to remain upright.

"Three-fifty, *Dave*." There's that menacing expression on his face again.

"$350 it is," you say swallowing hard and reaching into your pocket. There's a ratchet sound and you look up to find the pistol in your face.

"Shit!"

"Whoa, whoa, Dave! Cash or credit?" Scuzzbucket laughs loudly. " I'll need two forms of ID, including a driver's license, and I can write you up a receipt." He's still laughing. "I love doing that."

You reach for the wad of cash with the gun trained on you. "Count it out and put it on the tailgate. Can you handle the fear, Dave?"

"Be calm."

"Don't tell me how the fuck to be, *Dave!* We both know that ain't your *fuckin'* name! You do what the fuck I tell you." And now the pistol is tight against your torso, pressed against your heart.

"I don't want any trouble. You've got your money."

"There's no time to think when you've got 'em in your sights. It's time to pull the trigger, and the only thing you want is for your problem to go away—dead." Scuzzbucket points the pistol at his temple and you step back.

"It's OK, man."

"Can you handle the fear? The scariest sound in the world is the hammer clicking against a dud round. It's a *click* when what you need is a *bang*."

"I—"

"What's that, Captain Clay Sonnering of RASH Airlines?" You realize you've been made. Your anxiety ratchets up a notch and you're finding it hard to breathe.

"You've got your money. Can I get the gun?"

"Can I get the gun?" he says, mocking you. "The money in your pocket! And I'll take that watch, too. Set it on the ground and step the fuck back." There's the menace in his eyes.

"Can I keep the wat—"

"Set your fucking shit down on the ground and get the fuck out of here!" he says.

You take off the Submariner, a gift to you from yourself a dozen years ago and set it in the dirt—worth about $15,000 in today's money. The wad of twenties scrunched in your pocket lands on the ground next to it—the total haul not bad for a desert gun deal gone bad.

"Hey, Captain! Tell the cops you were trying to buy an illegal gun off a con by the roadside when you got robbed. I'm sure they'll help!" He laughs loudly.

You walk to the car with the gun trained on you, sit inside, and pull the door shut. The engine turns over with a roar and the heater blasts icy wind in your face. You blanche at the arctic blast and take one last look at Scuzzbucket as you turn off the dirt path and head back for the highway.

9

YOU TASTE HER, AND YOU rationalize it. It's custom, you tell yourself. Courtesy. And she's not bad really—a bit more wild down there than you expected—but still beautiful. Now she's moaning on the couch with breaths staccato and shallow.

Her sounds are flattering, but they grate on you because she's loud like a porno blaring at full volume in your ear, and her sounds seem disproportionate to your efforts. You're good at this, but not *that* good, and you wonder if all of her vocalizing is a show for an audience of one.

Her hips arch, and she shudders against your tongue, then grips your shoulders and cries out. And you consume her.

So you ask her to quiet down, take it down a notch for all parties involved. But she either can't hear you or won't obey, and now she's narrating her erotic journey like a baseball announcer doing the play by play. But she's still so loud—*so goddamn loud*—so you shove a hand over her mouth to stifle her cries because you don't want someone to think you're murdering her in here.

Still, her sounds feed your ego, and it's nice knowing you can still do this to a girl at your sun-damaged age. You've transported her to a land of milk and honey—a place with white knights, rainbows, and unicorns. You slay another dragon, and she cries out.

There's a small pulse in the distance like an ocean swell. It builds inside her, then crests and roars through her body as it crashes ashore. She cries out—and you consume her.

She's begging you now and tells you she doesn't want to come again. She mustn't, she says, but she's panting and moaning with her hips in your hands. She doesn't want to climb the mountain. She doesn't want to teeter on the edge and fall into the abyss. She doesn't want to die another little death.

So you kill her again.

You push her over the precipice until she cries out and falls like a pebble into the void. And you devour her death and say goodbye.

• • •

I'm aware of my strong sexual appetite, but I wouldn't call it anything more than that—it's an appetite. I'm not an addict or one of those TV characters in denial who mumble, "I don't have a *phrblrmeb* drinking problem!" before falling down a flight of stairs. But, I hide my strong sexual desire because it doesn't conform with my public persona.

Sex isn't addictive, because it's not harmful to its practitioners. Sex doesn't take the wheel of a three-thousand-pound vehicle and barrel into oncoming traffic, taking innocent lives with it. It doesn't gamble away the rent money or score drugs behind roadside bars. Sex is at the core of every man, from pool boy to prime minister, so why should I be judged negatively for my desire?

I like women is all, and I'd never describe my romantic interludes using slang—boning, banging, boffing, shagging, nailing, fucking—because I like women. Women can be loving and supportive, which is why I don't demean my experiences with them. What's fun about that? Sex isn't about conquests or high-fives in my book. It's about the comfort and connection of shared touch.

Naturally, I don't advertise my strong sexual desire because I don't need the raised eyebrows, like a married man announcing a trip to Thailand to "explore its natural beauty." So, I court my female companions on the DL and throw people off the scent with a few small lies.

I know my sexual peccadillos don't mean I have problems of willpower or character, but I wish I could turn off my negative self-talk. My self-loathing is world-class compared to the judgment I might hear from a professional. Yes, I've used sex to self-soothe, but what other method would you suggest? Between the stress of my career, gossipy coworkers, and running a home, it's hard to find solace. Sex. Food. Alcohol. Drugs. Travel. Extreme sports. Nicotine. Porn. Internet. Shopping. Work. Gambling. Video games. TV. All of it's self-medicating.

You may look at my current behavior and try to divine its source by looking at my past, but I'd rather not go there. I'm sure you mean well, but I don't need your analysis and would prefer it if you deployed your insights elsewhere.

In fact, I've made it a habit *not* to look back because even a small glance in my rearview mirror brings up a well of grief and no new insights. And if I've learned anything in my forty-three years on earth, it's that raking the muck of the past only gives you dirty fingernails and a sore back.

People talk about forgiveness, but few know that men forget and never forgive. Forgiveness is a Hollywood myth, after all, and persists because people have fallen for a fantasy version of reconciliation.

I understand the fascination with Hollywood because it's our chief mythmaker and we turn to it in times of need. But you have to remember, these are the same guys who brought us myths like *Love will find you*, *The good guy always wins*, and *Honesty is the best policy*. Hollywood's track record is spotty, so it's best to be skeptical of its offerings.

The forgiveness myth always starts out with a private conversation where two or more people sit down, often with the aid of a professional. The therapist adjusts the volume of venom between the parties so a dialogue can begin and enforces the rules of engagement: no anger, no blame.

But this is a Hollywood myth, so every word comes right from the script. There are no disagreements without insights, and everything proceeds in a spirit of cooperation. Yes, the sit-down is emotional, and facial tissue is consumed like napkins at a barbeque joint, but eventually there's peace.

There's a metaphorical sunrise on the horizon and it's all because of you, you amazing human! You were brave and faced the ones who hurt you because you knew it would be worth it. And guess what? It was! You told the truth, and you can't believe you weren't victimized (again) for sharing the sordid details. And there's more good news. The mythical sit-down is so productive you'll never have to open your mailbox and find another typewritten letter about the events of the past.

HELLO. WE HOPE YOU ARE WELL. WE DO NOT
RECALL ANY OF THE EVENTS YOU DESCRIBED
AND WE ARE UNABLE TO CONFIRM ANY OF YOUR
CHILDHOOD MEMORIES. YOU ARE ENTITLED TO
YOUR FEELINGS, OF COURSE, AND WE DO NOT
JUDGE YOU NEGATIVELY FOR THEM, BUT WE
THINK YOU HAVE A MENTAL HEALTH PROBLEM.
HAVE YOU CONSIDERED TALKING WITH A
THERAPIST?

WE LOVE YOU VERY MUCH AND ARE SO PROUD
OF YOU! WE THINK YOU ARE SUCH A NICE
PERSON AND WE ARE SORRY YOU ARE SO
ANGRY. MAYBE YOUR PROBLEMS ARE DUE TO
YOUR DEPRESSION AND ANXIETY. WE LOVE YOU
SO MUCH AND ALWAYS WILL. MUCH LOVE.

The forgiveness myth is powerful because it perpetuates
the idea that anything can be solved by a quiet talk in a
room decorated in earth tones. But if that were true, the
parents of unarmed youth murdered by police could
forgive the offending officers in a therapeutic hour and be
home in time for dinner.

But you're inside a Hollywood myth, so let's get back to
the sit-down.

The truth is welcome, and you can't believe your ears.
"You're right," says one of them. "Your memories are as
accurate as a Swiss watch," says the other. "We're sorry we
damaged your reputation, but we didn't want anyone to
know the truth. We lied about your mental health, your
motives, and your actions to ruin you before you could
speak up. Yes, we destroyed you personally and
professionally and isolated you from everyone you loved,

but we didn't mean anything by it. Why are you so angry?"

You can't believe they validate what you've been saying all along, and you want to shout it from the rooftops: "See! I was right. They were lying, and I told the truth." And there's no time to waste because you want your friends and family who have been led astray back pronto. You want your reputation back, and this is your comeuppance. Redemption!

You envision the sit-down's result like a not-guilty verdict at the end of a court trial, with everyone rushing over to your side of the table. You picture people crying as they line up to hug you and shake your hand. You imagine hundreds of letters from the very people who doubted you. "We're sorry," the letters read. "We should have believed you. We could've done more."

You imagine coming home to a phone that doesn't stop ringing, each call someone apologizing for their snap judgment. "I'm sorry. I can't believe I was tricked," they say. "I understand," you say, holding the phone close. But now you're slumped on the floor, tears streaming down your cheeks, knees in your chest, tight like a ball. "Apology accepted. Can we please move on?"

You're exhausted and spent because your redemption has been the hardest battle you ever fought. "Now," you wheeze to the caller on the line's other end, "Would you please be my friend and hold me close? Can I be a part of your loving family so I can go home? I'm so lonely, and I'd do anything for a friend. Please?"

And now you're crying and hyperventilating, lying on the floor. You can't stop sobbing because you've been buried in a mountain of shame and sadness you thought you'd never break through.

But now you're back at the mythical sit-down, the words have been said, and the calm has set in. It's time for the hug that shows you're moving on—but what, exactly, are you moving on *to*? To more twice-weekly therapist appointments at $200 a pop? To the fear of suffocation that fills your thoughts every time you drift off to sleep? To the flashbacks of blunt force trauma and sharp objects piercing your skin? To a medicine cabinet bursting with anxiolytics, pain killers, and pharma's best sellers?

"Sorry about your lifetime of psychological and medical problems," your transgressors say. "But look at the bright side, we're moving on!" Even the therapist leans over and offers her own take on the proceedings: "Try to forget the past. And don't think too much about the future either," she says.

But it's time to break bread and boy, are you hungry. There's a free meal in your future, and it's their treat! What a meal this is, you say tearing into food and drink. There's conversation and laughter, and it's time to mend fences. How's the house in Princeton, you ask? Marlene and Adam? Karla's flower store? How were Madagascar and Berlin? So many stories of careers, travel, marriages, children, and houses bought and sold.

The forgiveness myth spreads like cancer because we can't acknowledge horror without hope. We can't hear a sad story without a happy ending because it confirms a truth we'd rather not believe. So, we call on Hollywood to recast our horrors for public consumption.

All it takes is a screenwriter and a few suits around a table to transform a genocide into a love story with a handsome hero and an aid worker with a perfect body and a low-cut top. Racist police departments are reimagined with a lone wolf cop who protects the victim and ensures justice is done. Anything unpleasant is rewritten and recast so we can face our inhuman condition.

And yet the Hollywood myths persist: *The boy gets the girl, The hero gets his redemption, Hard work is rewarded, Evildoers get justice in the end, Love finds us all.* Hollywood lies, and we are complicit in the bargain because we are starved for hope.

Hope propels us forward during times of despair by telling us happiness lies over yonder. That if we have faith, we'll find romance, fulfillment, and success very soon. And yet, no one speaks of optimism's danger.

Too much hope takes your eye off the ball of daily living and prevents you from enjoying the present. It takes you away from art and culture and conversation and the beauty of a sky full of stars. Hope removes you from the present and puts your focus on a future date as yet undetermined. Blind optimism is like putting half of your salary in a bank account with plans to use it upon your death.

10

"THAT'S THE ONLY ENTRANCE RIGHT there," Katrina said, nodding to the W. 44th Street hotel and the outdoor carpeting leading to its front doors. The hotel was wrapped in a wainscoting of black granite and brass, and its windows revealed a lobby brimming with travelers.

But right now, the hotel was notable for the activity that hummed around its perimeter, where dozens of security barricades had been set up. NYPD uniforms and Secret Service were busy screening guests and directing traffic away from the hotel.

"Classic hotel setup. A single revolving door in the center and double doors on each side," Katrina said.

"Bloody hell, love. It's ugly as fuck."

"Were you expecting swans and a lake? It's Times Square."

The trio had found street parking on the north side of Eighth Avenue, and their vantage point conferred clear sight lines to the front doors. The group's car was so close to the hotel, in fact, they were within earshot of the activity out front if the wind blew just right.

Katrina twisted her shoulders and alternately looked at the security setup and down at the notes on her tablet. She and Sumito were in front, like that day at JFK, and Petrova was in back with her hands on a laptop. The only sounds inside the car were the clacking of keys and Sumito's groans when he lifted his buttocks and passed gas.

Out front, bellmen hailed cabs and loaded luggage as more barricades were set up and agents conferred with NYPD. Occasionally, a hotel guest would look up at the gray afternoon, as if wondering whether a downpour might spoil their day's plans. But this scene wouldn't play out much longer, not if Secret Service kept tightening its grip on vehicle traffic and pedestrians.

"Protectees usually get a private entrance, so I'm surprised the advance team chose this place," Katrina said. "Maybe it was pre-cleared: water, sewer controls, HVAC, telephony, networks, and conduit checked and sealed. They usually select more robust bunkers."

"Let's hit him in his SUV, love. We park a truck outside, wait for the motorcade to pass, and *boom*. Obliterate him and everything within a block," Petrova said.

"Inelegant but effective," Sumito said.

"Pull a Timothy McVeigh, kill hundreds of innocent people, and *then* get the death penalty?" Katrina swiped through a PDF on her tablet. "We need to take the Secretary alive."

The personnel outside the hotel included not just Secret Service and NYPD, but also a bomb squad, Strategic Response Group, counterterror, and personnel from the mayor's office. There were already a half-dozen bulletproof

SUVs on the street, and the Secretary of Defense hadn't yet arrived.

"That's it, love! We shoot him when he emerges from the motorcade and walks inside."

"Brilliant, Pet. We die in a hail of NYPD and Secret Service bullets in a Times Square blood bath. *Arigatou*, but no *arigatou*," Katrina said.

"So what is your fucking plan, love?"

"No bombs. No guns. The plan is *the plan*," Sumito said.

"One rifle shot to the head and we're done. I'll do it," Petrova said.

"What part of 'take him alive' don't you understand? Besides, over watch is already set up anywhere you could get a shot off. They're on top of every parking structure, apartment building, and hand job parlor."

"The Americans?" Sumito said.

"The entire bloody cavalry. They're probably watching us right now," Katrina said.

"You disgust me!" Sumito said, and Katrina blanched. He had his phone in his lap and looked up from the screen. "Manchester City whipped West Ham 5-0. *Cunts*...Look, let's not cock up here like we did in the subway." He looked Katrina in the eye and she, in turn, looked to Petrova.

"We'll need everything sorted when we come back, Pet."

"I'll have it, love."

"Everything, Petrova."

"I'll have it," the Hillingdon girl said with her face buried in her laptop.

"*Everything*, Pet."

"I said I'll have it!" Petrova stared at Katrina. "Now sod off."

Katrina sighed. "The Secret Service has made things considerably harder. I'm not showing up here with my tits in my hands."

Sumito huffed and looked out the window. "I think we can agree your performance in the subway was lacking."

"The teenager prevented me from placing the charge. What was I supposed to do? Kill her? The outcome was regrettable but unavoidable," Katrina said.

"Did she stop you? Or did you pussy out?" Sumito said.

"Bollocks. I made the call as I saw fit."

"Any obstacle can be overcome," Sumito said, bringing his face within inches of Katrina's. His sour breath overwhelmed her, and she fought back a gag. Tiny hairs sprouted from his nostrils and ears, and she felt certain she would vomit. "Try harder next time," he said in a foul plume, then returned to the driver's seat. Katrina exhaled relief and quickly rolled down her window.

Petrova looked up from her work. "RASH is badly damaged online and we're poisoning the web as you requested."

"You made your point at the terminal," Katrina said.

"Let's be clear. Neither of you set the goals for the team. *I do*. Capturing the Secretary will force the administration to go aggressive on terror and *voilà*, oil prices rise. We're long on oil futures, and as other airlines struggle to survive, Swoosh shall flourish."

"Look!" Petrova pointed across the street.

A Secret Service agent smiled and waved at a group of pedestrians as they approached the hotel. "Hi there, folks! Can you do me a favor and use the sidewalk on other side of the street? Thank you kindly." Another agent flagged a couple walking hand-in-hand with the same patter, then waved goodbye to them like a parent to a child.

Katrina nodded in the direction of the military-looking strike force out front with their body armor, helmets, and M4 carbines at the ready.

"Hawkeye travels with the Secretary of Defense at all times. They're unique to executive-level protectees because they run offense for the close protection team. If there's an attack, they'll coordinate a counterstrike, engage the target, and flank them while the close protection team gets the protectee to safety."

The agents continued working the security barriers like overeager club promoters, smiling and chatting with passersby. Another group of pedestrians walked toward the hotel, and an agent turned them away with the same overly polite faux friendship from behind his sunglasses.

"The Secret Service looks capable, but they're too encumbered to do anything. Each agent has a sidearm with extra magazine, a backup weapon, handcuffs, encrypted radio with battery, an earpiece, and microphone. And a few are carrying machine guns. And they're all wearing suits and ties in their dress shoes."

"Who's up for a shoe sale? I know I am," Petrova said.

"They're armed babysitters and PR flacks for the executive branch, with their toothy grins and aviators," Katrina said. "Look, here we go again."

"Hi there, folks! Would you guys mind walking around and using the other sidewalk?" the agent repeated as if reading from a script. Katrina huffed. "Thank you very much, folks. Have a good day!"

"Human shields. Nothing more."

"They have better equipment and training and an arsenal of guns," Petrova said.

"What are they gonna do? Hose down an entire block with automatic weapon fire? Murder dozens of innocent people? They're too scared because they've been over-trained."

"Hi there, folks! Hi!" another agent said with a wave and smile to some passersby. "Watch the traffic when you cross the street! Thanks so much!"

"Pathetic...I'm not sure about this one. They've got this place tight like a prom dress," Sumito said.

"But there's one thing the Secret Service can't do," Katrina said.

"What's that, love?"

"We'll use the quick-don respirators on our way back after we release the sarin. Then we grab the Secretary, get the hell out, and meet back at the RV. That's how we do it," Sumito said.

"When you say 'we,' you mean 'us,' right?" Petrova said. "Katrina and me? Just say 'you and Katrina,' OK?"

"*Fwoomp!* That's the sound the quick-don masks make when they attach to your face. They form a seal and then there's a *thhhk!* sound as the oxygen begins to flow. Don't take off the masks no matter what. Remember, *fwoomp!* and *thhhk!* Only the masks can keep you alive," Sumito said.

"Wait for me to signal it's all clear before you take off your mask," Katrina said.

"Love, you said the Secret Service has one thing they can't do. What's that?"

Katrina huffed. "They don't know how to be assholes."

"There's some unfinished business. I'll need both of you to accompany me as we pay a visit to a certain friend of Captain Clay Sonnering." The women nodded their heads.

11

THERE'S NO EASY DRIVING IN Manhattan, no boulevards for swallowing up miles at a time on the way to a destination. Sure, the West Side Highway and the FDR will get you up to highway speed, but they're inconvenient routes to the heart of the city. Here, the streets and avenues are saddled with stoplights and crosswalks every few hundred feet that will impede your forward movement.

Now, the subway bisects the street grid, and it can get you somewhere faster, which is the reason even the wealthy use the dilapidated trains that connect the city like blood vessels. The trains may be patched together with electrical tape and extension cords, but they're the fastest way to travel.

The Manhattan street grid system has never worn well on you because inefficiency is anathema to aviation. Commercial flying was founded on expediency, and no carrier seeks out longer routes because they know the impact on profits, crew, and equipment. Besides, no passenger would voluntarily fly from LGA to LAX *via the Canadian territories* unless they were out of their mind. Sure, pilots will occasionally take a circuitous route when weather, air traffic, and contingencies dictate, but never without reason.

In Manhattan, you're subservient to the grid, and the grid you must obey. But, the street grid is your enemy when you're late because you can't *make time*, like ducking through a neighbor's yard during a walk to get someplace faster.

It was Mr. Stewart, your middle school math teacher, who taught you about right triangles and the shortest distance between two points. And now, you'd kill to honor his memory and grab a hypotenuse to speed your walk to Deanna's on 48th Street.

The incident at JFK was resolved successfully, your suspension is over, and you've been back in the cockpit for a month now. But, tonight, you landed at LaGuardia late, which means you're late for your date, huffing as you head north to 48th and 11th from Port Authority. You wish you could bulldoze a diagonal from where you are now to Deanna's door, flattening the tons of concrete, steel, rebar, brick, and mortar to get to there faster—because she's horny.

Right now is the sweet spot, the time of night when she's had a few glasses of wine and is feeling good. Deanna's been texting you since you landed, telling you what she wants you to do to her and how, and although a hookup isn't the most noble reason for a date, at least she's honest.

But you want to arrive at her place soon, because it won't be long till she sets her jaw and the anger settles in. She'll grow sullen, the bloom will be off the rose, and you'll become a target. You want to be gone long before that happens, avoiding what would otherwise be a narrow escape—pants buttoned in the hallway, shirt barely on, shoes in hand as you dash for the elevators. You want to be gone before the accusations fly amid the occasional physical object—way before that.

It's warm out. The uniform tie hangs loosely off your shirt collar, and the white dress shirt is pasted to your skin, sticky with sweat. You're *schvitzing* with sweat dripping down your flanks and pits and want to peel off your uniform and soak in a cool tub.

The navy jacket is draped over your shoulder as you look left and right on 47th so you don't get creamed by a cab. There's a playground up ahead and a small joy in your heart because taking the shortcut will put you within a minute of Deanna's door.

The play structures loom like multi-colored obelisks, and a single floodlight shines into the playground's center. But at this hour, the place is barren, with no kids on the swings or courts and no parents in sight.

You enter the playground and a chain-link fence rattles loudly in front of you as a teen walking by the north entrance smashes its mesh. His eyes find yours, and he looks at you in your suit and tie walking through the small lot. His fist slams into the fence again, and he turns left into the playground from the north side.

The lanky boy walks like a panther with his head held high and shoulders shifting sharply to and fro. He's wearing a blue hoodie, striped tennis shoes, and a red logo cap that sits askew on his head. There's a snarl on his face, and you wonder why a kid like that is filled with such anger. He doesn't look like he has any reason to be mad, and yet you feel your skin prickle.

He turns around, looking behind and then back in your direction, and stretches his back. You're both headed to the playground's center on a collision course, but you avoid eye contact because you know nothing good ever comes from that. But you're curious about the teen—fascinated, even—as if he were some sort of case study on urban youth.

The teen has a muscular build for such a small frame and is *jacked* for his age, with strong arms and broad shoulders. And now he's moving forward with more locomotion, more purpose, as he passes the monkey bars, owning every step of the way. His fists are clenched tightly at his sides, and you swear you can hear his rapid breathing.

You near the playground's center and notice his expression isn't anger at all, but menace, because his lips are pressed tight and he's hyperventilating like he's preparing for battle. And it's this moment you realize your grave mistake. *Fuck. FUCK! Is it too late to run?*

Your only options are to continue straight ahead or turn and run full tilt, because it's about to be confrontation time. But, you're no slouch—you could fight and you weren't a bad scrapper in your day, either. You could hold your own if need be, plus you don't want to be thought a coward.

The two of you pass each other in the playground's center, with him on the left and you on the right. There's a small head nod as you look each other in the eye. And there's nothing. No confrontation. No problems. Nothing.

The air is sucked from your lungs and you crumple in a heap as a sharp punch hits your Adam's apple. Your luggage and laptop clatter to the pavement and you taste gravel in your mouth. The shock to your system is so severe that there's no pain, but you're instantly disabled. The paralysis hits you like a lightning bolt, and you gasp, hissing, struggling for air.

The teen cocks his fist and bends over you, ready to send a punch to your face. He snarls and strikes, and you turn your head at the last second so his fist smashes asphalt. You catch your breath in time to groan and taste blood leaking from your nose.

There's a crack as a board smashes the teen hard in the head, spraying blood across his face. He topples onto the ground next to you with saliva gurgling from his lips. A foot kicks him hard in the back of the head and he's spitting up blood.

"Monkey bar motherfucker!" a voice says.

There's a dribble of blood as the teen coughs up a tooth inches from your face, and you wince in pain. Hands are in the boy's pockets, removing a gun and wad of cash, all of it stuffed into a black roller bag. There are a few more kicks to the teen's body and his breaths are like a faint whistle.

"Listen up, motherfucker," a voice says. "The name's Varsick, got it? V-A-R-S-I-C-K. Sam Varsick. That's the guy's name who just kicked your fucking ass! Come and find me, motherfucker, and I'll finish what I started. *All right?!*"

You look up to find the portly figure of Sam Varsick cut in silhouette by the floodlight, huffing with chest rising and falling. Sam bends down to you, and now you're looking at his wrinkled face and seventies porn moustache.

"Jesus, Clay. You look like shit."

"How did you..." There's a sharp pain in your side. *"Shit!"*

"Listen, dickwad. You were talking a lot of shit on the descent even though I was a nice guy and let you land tonight. You looked like you were going to get fucked up tonight, so I followed you from the train."

"Thank you. I really appreciate—"

"Save the speech for the Oscars. Let's get the fuck out of here."

"I just—"

"Rise and shine. Come on. Get up." He reaches down with a hand, and you limp to your feet. He keeps his hand under your armpit, supporting you as you take a few steps.

"Great news about Blancando, by the way," Sam says.

"HazMatt? What?" you wheeze.

"I got an email from Operations. Blancando made senior captain," he says.

"*He what*?!" you say.

"Matt Blancando. He made Senior Captain," Sam says.

"Are you kidding me!?"

"Weird as fuck. I don't know what's going on at RASH these days. Getting promoted from first officer to senior captain. That shit never happens."

Sam wipes his shoes with a handkerchief and throws the wooden board to the side. "Some dumbshit left his skateboard here. Lucky for you, dickwad."

There's the sound of sirens in the distance. "Come on. Let's get the fuck out of here. You can walk. *Easy does it.*" He reaches down and grabs your laptop and roller bag off the ground. "All you need is a Band-Aid and a stiff drink and you'll be good as new. Cowboy up. We can split the cash I took off the fucker at the bar."

"What about him?" I say looking at the teen lying motionless on the ground.

"*What about him*? Come on," Sam says.

"I know, but—"

"So, dickwad..." Sam says.

"*What?*"

"You need a gun?"

12

I'M A BIT OF A softie, even childlike, and I'm ashamed to admit I like the things that make any four-year-old smile. I love kids, hugs, puppies, and birthday cake, and I can't see my priorities changing anytime soon. Love and touch are my favorites because they renew my spirit, and I'm trying to reconcile these rarest of male traits.

I love the kindergartners in my neighborhood because their innocence reminds me of childhood's joys. I'm talking about the littlest of the little ones, heading off to school in their oversize ladybug and dinosaur backpacks like miniature soldiers on the move. I like knowing these kids' days are filled with music and story time, cupcakes and potty breaks—the basics of a happy childhood. And I get emotional seeing them with their parents, because it reminds me of love's power.

I realize I shouldn't love children so much, but I want to be clear on one thing: *I don't love kids that way.* I have no desire to be alone with children, not now or ever, and would never hurt or victimize them. That's not me at all.

HazMatt says the reason I'm so sensitive is because I had too much female nurturing growing up and that I'll need to toughen up if I want a good woman. Women don't go for that male sensitive shit, he says, so I need to stop being a "beta" and embrace my inner asshole.

I've always had difficulty with male pursuits, especially aggression and romance, and I've made little progress in these areas since my teens. It's hard for me to be either dominant or dashing, and as a result, I fail at both. And that's why now, at the bar, I'm HazMatt's punch line.

"So Clay sucked my dick!" Matt says.

The tall blonde doubles over laughing, sloshing her rum and coke, while the California Girl leans on me for support. The twentysomething women contort like seizure patients in fits of laughter that fill the Chelsea lounge.

Alexa, the blonde, comes up for air, wipes the mascara from her eyes, and leans on Matt's bicep. "Oh my god! Did you make that up? That's the funniest thing I've ever heard!" Her plum lips near Matt's ear whisper something to him as her hand roams his muscly arm.

All's well in the world because Matt's *target* is now hanging on him, and that means I did my job. I don't mind being Matt's punch line as long as he gets what he wants, but I wish I could take credit for the women talking with us. Except I didn't do a thing—Matt was running a *routine*.

"What happened to you?" the California girl says touching the bruises on my face.

"I–"

"You should see the other guy," Matt says and the women laugh.

Binomial nomenclature is what it's called, but it has nothing to do with the taxonomy of species. It's a bar pickup routine, a rehearsed set of dialogue and jokes, designed to seduce women. Matt found the seduction move on the Dark Web, and he uses it to bag prey at bars in the city. This particular routine is a long joke, and it uses my mouth on his penis as the punch line for a disgusting ten-minute story.

Everything about *binomial nomenclature* is blue, and when I say "blue," I'm putting it mildly. The joke is so foul it'd make a Marine blush. It contains copious amounts of fisting, defecation, ejaculation, felching, masturbation, necrophilia, and ethnic stereotypes. It's also shown a remarkable ability for getting women from the bar to the bedroom.

My theory is the joke works on bar women precisely because it's so foul. Drunk women, in particular, are attracted to guys who use *binomial nomenclature* because it shows the joke teller is an alpha male. The joke is so disgusting that only a strutting, loud-talking, arrogant man would ever tell it—and these are types of men drunk women find sexy.

HazMatt and possibly Pharm Boy or Microfiber, two other friends of ours whom Matt has given nicknames, are the only guys who could use *binomial nomenclature* and get away with it. The joke is shocking, yes, but if you're brave enough to tell it, you're often rewarded with female company.

HazMatt looks over at me with a cocked eyebrow and leads Alexa to the back of the bar while the California Girl toys with her hair and checks her phone.

"Is he always that funny?" the California Girl says with her face in her phone.

"Yep, pretty much always."

The faint figures of Matt and Alexa are visible in the distance. Alexa wraps her hands around Matt's neck as he encircles her with his arms. She pulls back, smiling, and he moves in for a kiss. His cowboy hat lands on her head, and his voice is in her ear. She laughs, slapping his chest. Alexa kisses him again and walks back toward us, trying hard to contain her glee.

"It was nice meeting you guys," she says with a smile, and with that, she grabs her purse and heads back to HazMatt and her adventure.

"Alexa likes Matt," the California Girl says.

"I got that impression."

I wanted to congratulate HazMatt on his promotion to senior captain, but mostly I wanted to know how he got the promotion so quickly and without going through the usual channels—but this isn't the time or place. For now, I need to put that aside and focus on learning about women. He and I can always catch up later.

I realize this scene must look juvenile to you, and you probably think I enable Matt's bar pickups, but I'd prefer it if you withheld judgment. You may even wonder what Matt's doing picking up women when he's got a girlfriend already. I don't know the answer to that, but I let him manage his personal affairs rather than risk our friendship over a difference in morals. And, really, who am I to say what's right? It's not like I'm a shining example of good judgment when it comes to women.

I'm grateful that HazMatt—well all three of them, including Pharm Boy and Microfiber—have taken me under their wings. Tonight, you could call me a wingman or helper as the guys go about their bar seductions. Pharm Boy's real name is Phil, and he works in pharmaceutical advertising. Microfiber's name is Roger, and he works in fashion in the Financial District, but they prefer I use their sobriquets when we're together.

"Matt and Alexa are going to another bar together. Do you wanna hang here or go somewhere else?" the California Girl says.

"Will you be OK getting home?" I say.

"Oh...I thought we could...I was hoping we could maybe hang out some more?" she says with a friendly smile.

"I don't know. It's getting kind of late." I walk over to Pharm Boy and see what he's up to.

The guys say I need to power up my dating and get some *game*. I need to start denying women's requests and be meaner to them, because that will increase my sex appeal. I should hide my sensitivities because women prefer hyper-masculinity. So, I've taken up boxing and am learning to be more aggressive, eschewing the sensitive for the sensual. I'm learning to bluster, to take up more space, to snarl to get my point across—and people are noticing. I never, ever, want to be thought of as sensitive, because I know that's death for any man.

"The girls love this shit," Pharm Boy whispers in my ear. He can't stop complimenting himself because the bar women are loving his magic tricks and sleight of hand. He says the illusions are making them wet.

"Dude, *binomial nomenclature* never fails," he says. "See her?" He points to a blonde in a leopard-print dress that Matt and I were talking to earlier. "Maybe I'll be her next mistake."

"I don't know," I say.

I head back to California Girl, grab a seat across from her, and see what she's up to.

• • •

You sit across from her listening politely because that's what you do on a date, and you want to get to know her in the fashion she expects. And that's what this is, right? *A date.* You even wore a sport coat and dress shoes to spiff up your drab attire in an effort to impress. Still, it's a little odd sitting across from her, because she's only in town for a few nights.

But she seems happy enough in your company, if a little nervous, with a warm smile and long black hair that sweeps across her shoulders every time she laughs. *Of course she's a brunette.* The chief problem, however, is her outfit, which is right for all the wrong reasons.

The white, form–fitting three–quarter sleeve body con dress has a bamboo motif and fits her like a showgirl's leotard. Faint yellow leaves and emerald stalks drape across her toned physique, and her curves stir your carnal desire. The magenta lipstick and black heels she's selected complement the outfit perfectly, but they only add to your distraction. You're trying hard to focus on the words coming from her mouth, but you're overwhelmed by the shock of feminine pulchritude. *What a beautiful brunette.*

The California Girl is actually a better fit in the humming Chelsea hotspot than you are because her style matches the swanky interior. The zebra–striped bar and cow–print booths are illuminated in colored spotlights, giving the lounge a hyper–sexualized Flintstones' vibe. People engage in staccato conversations and pretend they're not on the hunt as house music thrums. But now, California Girl is complaining to you about the noise and tells you she can't hear over the din.

So, she asks if it'd be OK to share your side of the booth, and to that request you nod your head. And now her body is tight against your side and you inhale deeply to further your intoxication. She rests a hand on your thigh as she talks, and the shock of warmth makes your pulse pound like an anxiety attack.

It was only a few months back that you and HazMatt walked into the San Francisco hotel after the first leg of your turn. It was an unremarkable check-in, one of thousands of your career, and you were only there to rest before a 7:15 AM return the next day. But you were in uniform, and that always attracted some attention, especially from women.

The California Girl struck up a conversation with you by the hotel elevators—HazMatt took his cue and peeled right for the bar. There was some friendly chitchat, she smiled and asked many questions while touching your arm. "I'm only in town a few nights on business, but let's have a drink," she'd said. You said nothing in return, but nodded and smiled because you were friendly and people were calm in your company—even your mother said so.

The female stranger seemed harmless enough with her long black hair, petite frame, and youthful smile, but she was otherwise attached. "My boyfriend and I live in Santa Cruz. He works in finance at the same company as me." But the conclusion to the encounter was odd: she'd offered her phone number and you hadn't even asked. Still, you gave her your card because it was polite and professional decorum mattered.

How would you describe the encounter with the California Girl those months ago? Was there an expression for an encounter initiated by a woman where the man said so little? A friendly chat? A proposition? A lonely soul reaching out for company? Still, you'd put her number in your phone that night and imagined it would digitally decay like so many others.

But tonight she was in town on business, and her text had greeted you earlier in the day because she wanted to meet up. *Do you have time for a drink?* You'd agreed without hesitation and invited Matt along for the fun. You'd even suggested the spot, so you weren't naïve about the evening's plans.

Sitting here with her now, you watch the predators circling the periphery and surveying the night's offerings. They smile and laugh from behind their cocktails and shiny watches, fresh in button-down shirts and $100 haircuts, navigating the crowd with ease. They offer many shoulder touches and hand clasps as they work the room, but you know what they're about. They're liars, cheaters, and ne'er-do-wells, only here for an injured gazelle.

Now the California Girl is telling you a story about last night, and although the anecdote is interesting, it's no epic tale, so you respond with a little laugh and smile to encourage the proceedings. But is that what you want? For things to *progress*? Is there a goal except using her to quell your own pain?

Your hand lands on her bare thigh, and she neither protests nor removes it. It's a little touch, fairly chaste in its present location, and you hardly notice your faux pas until she pulls your hand higher on her leg and covers her lap with a napkin.

Your lips meet in a kiss, and she brings you inside her. She's warm and wet like liquid sunshine. Her taste is in your mouth, and you reach for the Napa Valley plonk beside you, a special suggested by the sommelier. The red wine is decent but no blockbuster, and you wonder whether the pour is "special" due to its markup or its abundance in the bar's dusty basement.

You wish you could say that any of this matters, but now that you're inside her you know what this is about. She's cute enough and you get the feeling you're equally special in her eyes, and that this scene has been played out before on her "business trips." You're her number twenty-three (or higher), and she's your number fifty-four, and on that count you're certain.

And now she's telling you how wasted she was last night—oh, god, how wrecked! She and her friends were doing Irish car bombs and Jaeger at Boots and then went to Wipalow and then finally to Folder on the Lower East Side. They wrapped things up at Kicks, and by then it was 3:15 A.M. and she knew she had to get back to her hotel to function today.

You feel like the jaded standup comic doing a thirty-minute set because you're not present, only phoning it in. The hack comic only cares about his pay, his drink, his fuck, and your goals are similarly pedestrian. It's not that you have no respect for her, it's that you have no respect for yourself. There's no intentional cruelty, because you didn't plan for things to go this way.

But with her now, it doesn't matter what you do as long as you don't throw up on your shoes. You're in, guaranteed—a hundred percent. So you nod affirmatively at her story, smile and laugh in all the right places.

And now the cab is lurching down 23rd Street as she's clutching your side and telling you about her relationship. Her boyfriend is her priority, she tells you, and she thinks they'll be engaged soon. "I love him with all my heart, so let's not do anything. Let's not go so fast. We can hang out and talk."

But her protests only raise your suspicions she's done this before. As if to prove the point, she removes her thong underwear and places it in your hands with a kiss. And now you're making out in front of the cabbie, and then the grope-fest continues outside your building.

"Maybe I could come up and get some coffee, OK?" she says.

"Sure. OK."

Power and authority work their charms, bringing them to you from around the globe. Soon she'll be upstairs with you, or you'll be at her place for whatever activity you desire. The sad thing is she's not even naked and you're already bored because your heart's not in it. You're nothing but a hack stand-up comic.

The comedian perfects the art of sending the crowd into fits of laughter and seconds-long applause breaks, and with it comes a newfound dislike. They say it happens because it's easy for them to manipulate the audience—that this power corrupts them. The comic becomes so good at what they do, they come to despise the very people they used to crave impressing.

13

THE TAXI, TAKEOFF, AND CLIMB out are over and it's time to enjoy the return from Miami against light blue skies. You departed the land of ass and alligators heading zero-three-five (northeasterly), at three-one-zero (31,000 feet), cruising at 476 mph. It's a near-perfect day for flying, and it feels good to be heading back to New York.

Contrails, plumes of cooled jet engine wake, surround you at several points on the clock face, evidence of other jets. These trails are proof of the marvel of ATC (air traffic control): that you can safely share the skies without risk of collision.

The streaks of white paint on the sky encourage you to search for planes, and if you're lucky, you may catch a sliver of silver as it roars past you in the blink of an eye. These aerial encounters are common but still arouse a tinge of terror in you, like an arrow zipping past your face at five hundred miles per hour.

The jets around you aren't threats to your collision bubble—the area that extends beyond the physical space of your plane—but there's no delicate way to put it: you want to avoid a midair collision. You're all in this together, from the pilots and controllers at ATC to the computers and collision avoidance technology—all of it designed to prevent such a potentiality.

"*RASH four-eight-seven, Miami center. Traffic, ten o'clock, thirteen miles, south-bound, climbing to flight level two-nine-zero,*" says a controller.

"RASH four-eight-seven, roger. Looking for the traffic," Matt says.

The ATC transmission tells you another jet is thirteen miles away and headed toward you in under one minute at an altitude of 29,000 feet—just below you. The advisory alone doesn't require action, but now the onboard TCAS, Traffic Alert and Collision Avoidance System, perks up with its computerized voice.

TRAFFIC, TRAFFIC, it says.

The TCAS warning means you must initiate a visual check to locate the intruder, so you and Matt look out the windows like a couple of kids in a tree fort hunting for the bully who just nailed you with an orange. The nomenclature for the approaching jet has also changed because it's violated your collision bubble. It's now an *intruder.*

"It's ten miles out and closing," Matt says. "At two-eight-oh and climbing at our eleven o'clock. *There,*" he says pointing out the window.

And now you've got eyes on him, too. The giant quadruple turbofan jet is the colossus of the skies, the largest passenger plane in operation. He's dragging four white contrails behind him like a set of fluffy cotton strings.

"Center, RASH four-eight-seven. Traffic in sight," you say and close the mic. The traffic display depicts the intruder as a yellow blip at the edge of a circle heading toward its center. "He's entering our envelope."

TRAFFIC, TRAFFIC, the computer says.

"Maintain three-one-zero, buddy boy. We're good."

"He's rising, sir. Twenty-eight and change."

The intruder is less than two skyscrapers beneath you and is rising to your flight level at subsonic speed.

"As he should. That's what ATC said."

TRAFFIC, TRAFFIC

"He's still rising, sir. Two-nine-zero and closing. Seven miles out."

"Stay calm, HazMatt. He's only a yellow blip on the display. We don't adjust course based on a yellow alert since he's forty to forty-five seconds out at his rate of climb. Wait for the action audible, the resolution advisory or R.A. If we get one, we'll move. The R.A. comes at twenty to twenty-five seconds to impact...Yellow means monitor. Red means move your ass."

"Roger that," Matt says.

"*Tau* is what they use to predict the intersection of flight paths based on collision envelopes, HazMatt. It's a mathematical value for the ratio of a circle's circumference to its radius for calculating range over range at speed. The distance to collision doesn't matter. It's about *time* to impact. TCAS tells you how long it will take him to enter your collision area using tau and other geometry based on the speeds and vectors of bo–"

TRAFFIC, TRAFFIC

"Where's he now, HazMatt?"

"Four NM out and closing. Flight level three-zero-zero."

"Stay put and listen to the comms and TCAS."

"Sir, he's at 30,000 feet, but Center said he wasn't going above two-nine."

"He's still a thousand feet underneath us. We're good...The TCAS calculation isn't time to actual skin on skin contact. We're in a dynamic collision envelope that changes in size based on our speed, altitude, and prox–"

"*RASH four-eight-seven, traffic alert! Turn left immediately, climb, and maintain three-three zero,*" says Center.

DESCEND, DESCEND, says the computerized voice of TCAS.

You disengage the autopilot and autothrottle and hear the "cavalry charge," the melodic chime reminding you the plane is under manual control.

"Center, RASH four-eight-seven. Unable to comply. We're getting a TCAS R.A," Matt says over the comms, then looks at you. "Sir, follow the TCAS R.A."

You elect to follow Center's direction, ignoring Matt and TCAS, and pull back on the stick, shoving the thrust levers forward given the urgency on the comms. The plane's nose pitches higher, and you hope you don't pull more than a quarter G because any gravitational force stronger than that will be felt by the cabin and raise their alarm.

"*RASH four-eight-seven, expedite climb! FL three-three-zero,*" says Center.

DESCEND NOW, DESCEND NOW, says TCAS.

"Descend, sir. Follow TCAS. He's bearing down on us."

You're in a tunnel of concentration and pull hard on the stick to climb higher and are certain this move will be felt by passengers. You're already dreading the muffled cries from the cheap seats, but reason your decision is better than a surprise from a one million pound visitor at 500 miles per hour.

A silvery wisp roars by underneath you, close enough for you to make out the tail number on the fuselage—if it wasn't moving so fast.

"*Fuck,*" Matt says.

"Shhh. Listen," you say.

"*RASH four-eight-seven, maintain three-three-zero,*" says Center.

CLEAR OF CONFLICT, says TCAS.

"RASH four-eight-seven, clear of conflict. Three-three-zero," Matt says, slumping in his seat.

A yellow strobe pulses, painting light outside the cockpit as an overhead light snaps on. There's the sound of shuffling paper behind you as an industrial motor starts up with a groan.

"Nice ride, boys. That'll do it for today," says a voice.

The pod at the top of the giant scissor lift jerks, then begins its slow descent like a children's amusement park ride. You, Matt, and a RASH Airlines examiner are belted inside a flying simulator the size of a children's bedroom, which is suspended dozens of feet in the air inside a warehouse at the Atlanta training facility.

"Very nice, indeed," the examiner says with a polite smile. "Once we reach the platform, would you please excuse us, Mr. Blancando?"

"Yes, sir." Matt unhooks his harness and waits for the capsule to stop moving. Finally, there's a jolt and a pneumatic hiss as it comes to a stop at a set of metal stairs. Matt places a hand on your shoulder as he walks out with a smile on his face.

"This will only take a moment of your time, Captain," the examiner says consulting his tablet computer. "Captain Sonnering, the tail strike in New York was resolved and you and Mr. Blancando were reinstated in its wake. Today's checkride was a controlled environment simulation so we could make a decision about future opportunities." There's a smile on his face as his eyes wander up and to the left as if searching for the right words.

"Let me be frank, Captain Sonnering. This wasn't acceptable performance for someone at your level. I'm very concerned by today's outcome and curious why you didn't you follow the R.A. from the collision avoidance computer over ATC. The Aeronautical Information Manual instructs airmen to follow R.A.s over controller directions when there's a conflict between the two."

You're listening to the examiner's words but find yourself yawning involuntarily and quickly cover your mouth. Over his shoulder and outside the pod, two figures are talking in the stairwell landing in the distance.

"R.A.s take priority because the computer has situational awareness, Captain. You follow TCAS until you're free of conflict and *then* resume direction from ATC. That last part you did correctly." You're still looking over his shoulder at something. "Captain, do I have your attention?"

"Sorry," you say looking him in the eye. "You do now."

You advocate for yourself in gentle tones, reminding him of Center's urgency in the hypothetical presented. He nods politely at your words like a Japanese businessman, but his expression doesn't change—so you press your case.

There was no imaginary near miss between aircraft, you argue. No risk of collision or injuries to passengers or crew.

You call attention to your medical and psychological recertifications done *after* the incident at JFK and show him you're the picture of health and wellness.

The examiner continues nit-picking your performance like a Monday morning quarterback, and that's when you realize what this is about. Your future at RASH Airlines is a *fait accompli* because management has already asked the simulation examiner to pull the trigger.

"Although we've decided to separate from you formally, we are encouraged by your professionalism and years of service. Mr. Sonnering, if you would please take the stairs to the first floor, a representative from Human Resources will meet you." He stands and extends a handshake, a polite smile on his face again. "Thank you, Mr. Sonnering."

"Is this? I don't underst—"

"Your position is being eliminated and we will be separating from you formally, Mr. Sonnering. Please. Take the stairs to the first floor." He points to the exit with an open hand. "Please."

"*Shit*," you say too loudly.

Your mouth is dry, and you want something to drink. *It's over? After everything I've done? Because of this? What about my years of accolades and spotless reviews?* You stand there frozen like a man who's been told of his spouse's death, trying to catch your breath.

"I know this will take some getting used to, and I know I speak for all of us in saying your service has been commendable." You're standing there slackjawed when you spot Matt outside the simulator talking to a man and gesturing like a mime to the faint sounds of laughter.

Matt appears to be pantomiming the simulator flight's last five minutes in a mockery of your actions. He makes the face you did when you responded to Center and does an exaggerated impression of your voice when you realized you were in over your head. He makes farting noises to pump up his comedy.

"I...Thank you," you say to the examiner as you try to make sense of the conversation in view. You exit the vestibule and clamber across the metal platform to find the two men conversing.

"What the hell is th–"

"Oh, hey!" Matt says to you. "Clay! I was...uh...This is Don Merselin, the VP of RASH Training here in Atlanta. Don Merselin, Captain Clay Sonnering."

"Nice to meet you, Captain," the VP says.

"And you...A moment of your time, Matt?" you say.

"Sure," he says.

"I need to make a call anyway. Captain Sonnering, nice meeting you," the VP says, heading down the stairs to his office.

"Hey, so I never got a chance to congratulate you on your promotion. I don't know how you did it, but you did. Congratulations on making senior captain, HazMatt."

"Thanks. It's been quite a journey," Matt says.

"Unfortunately, I got my ass handed to me."

"What? Shit, I'm so sorry," he says.

"All of these coincidences so close together, right? You make senior captain a few days before I'm fired. It's a strange world we live in," you say.

"I'm not sure I like your tone, Clay. What are you saying?" he says.

"*Nothing*. I can't believe you got the job I wanted. I had the experience for it, you knew I was applying for it, and yet here I am—and now you're king of the hill."

"Don't be so hard on yourself. Experience isn't about age. It's about mileage. I've done a lot in my career, and management took notice," Matt says.

"I watched that Swoosh Airlines announcement video you sent, but there was a woman in the audience that looked familiar to me. And that's when I compared her to the footage from one of my terminal cameras. Matt, she's the same woman I found hanging outside the RASH Operations Center before the terminal attack. It's *the same woman!* Maybe she has something to do with the bombing!"

"What? No way. You sure it's the same person?" he says.

"A hundred percent."

"Be careful. I wouldn't share what you have until you know for sure what you've got," Matt says.

"So what's this you've been doing out here while I've been getting fired? Another one of your bar routines?"

"I was joking, Clay. You're not so old you can't take a joke now, are you?"

"I'm not in a joking mood!"

"What do you want from me? Sympathy? After what you put me through? I'll bet you thought you were going to waltz in here doing your captain thing and get back online. Except I knew you were going to fuck it up, Clay, so I'm getting some distance from you," Matt says.

"Wow. The truth finally comes out."

"I'm not going down in flames with you. Not this time."

"Both of us were flying in there. You're my first officer."

"Correction—*I was*. Not anymore." he says.

"I lost my job! After two decades!"

"How do you think it reflects on me when my partner screws up a checkride? I'm *still* trying to crawl out from under your toxic shadow, and every day you make it harder. That's right—*you* make it harder. You made your bed and you can sleep in it."

"Fuck you."

"Say it again. I dare you," Matt says.

You bring your face to within inches of his and exhale on his skin. "*Fuck. You.*"

Matt swings at you but he's wide and off the mark, so you duck and clock him in the jaw with a roundhouse. He stumbles backward onto the ground, and the metal stairs rattle like a cage as he clutches his jaw and sets his gaze on you.

"You're done, you fucking asshole," he says. Matt stands and heads down the stairs and out of sight.

The security guards' hands are tight on your arms as you're frog-marched from the warehouse and into the parking lot. You're clutching a pile of paperwork in your hands, and the bright June sunshine hurts your eyes. You search your pockets for your sunglasses and car keys and feel your shirt already sticky with sweat from the humidity.

At the Atlanta airport, the next New York-bound flight isn't on RASH Airlines but on a budget carrier with a few seats left. You're no longer eligible for reciprocal free or low-cost "jumpseat" ticketing on RASH partner airlines, so you use your credit card and pay full price for a one-way ticket to LaGuardia.

The flight is leaving shortly, so you hustle to the gate and are given a throughway by Security, who spot the four stripes on your sleeve. You board the flight and find a seat in back by the galley. The gleaming new airliner has a tasteful and well-appointed interior, and you note the crew's well-tailored uniforms. You sink into a plush leather seat, and there's the faint smell of jasmine in the air as the crew distributes warm hand towels and snacks to boarding passengers. Their smiles convey an ease and even a pleasure in what they do. You wish you could bottle their pride and take it with you.

There's an announcement from the captain over the PA as he welcomes you aboard. You're ready to doze off by the time the captain finishes his monologue: "Well, folks, we invite you to sit back, relax, and enjoy the Swoosh Airlines experience."

14

THE HUMAN BODY IS STRONG and holds up with a little daily maintenance—bathing, brushing, flossing, exercise—basics to take care of the human machine. The body can endure pain and frustration, heartache and despair to survive like a tortoise until that final, inexorable breath. I know this from nineteen and a half hours spent on Russia's economy airline.

The trip began with a spur-of-the-moment impulse to see Plim and her wife, Randala, in West Bengal. This is the trip I pressured Plim into inviting me on those weeks ago when we were in Manhattan.

I know, I know. I'm not proud of foisting myself on her, and I know the move was selfish, but I was lonely and wanted to get away after losing my job. I was game for the trip in the abstract, but I hadn't really thought it through.

I'd been to India many times before, but these weren't cultural immersions with the people, merely layovers as part of my career. I was, and still am, an India *newbie* and knew I needed to bone up on the basics. Yes, I'd heard about the hospice volunteers in Kolkata and Mother Teresa's work with the poor, but only in a high-school textbook sort of way.

I wanted to do something, anything to get away because I was going bonkers without my job and figured a trip would clear my head. Maybe I'd do some sightseeing in India. That could be fun, relaxing even.

And that's how I ended up in front of my computer scrolling through fares from Russia's economy carrier on a sunny Saturday. I couldn't believe it when I found a $599 New York to Netaji Subhas Chandra Bose International Airport (Kolkata, West Bengal) round-trip departing the coming Tuesday. The flight fit the bill perfectly, so I snapped it up, figuring I could get some reading done on the long journey.

But after I entered my credit card information and checked out, I noticed a tiny phrase at the bottom of the screen that sent a chill down my spine: TOTAL TRIP TIME: 33H 30M (INCLUDING LAYOVERS). I'd be spending a lot of time sitting.

I boarded the Moscow leg at JFK the following week and had my travel bag dialed in perfectly. The Russian carrier served a nice dinner onboard, too. It was a "nice" dinner, but not "*nice* nice," like lobster and caviar. But the food was good enough—you know, serviceable—and I had a drink and watched a movie. The evening wore on and I even read for a little bit as we soared over the pole. But by then it was dark outside and I was ready for bed, so I took a sleeping pill for a night's rest in the skies.

You could say my plan worked like a charm because I woke the next morning refreshed. I wasn't rejuvenated like a night's sleep in my own bed, but I was rested enough, and ate breakfast and read some more. Later, I had lunch and finished my book, following that up with two more movies and the first few chapters of *another* book. I slept some more and woke up to discover we weren't halfway there.

I'd piloted these routes and knew the grind, so you'd think that would've prepared me for my role as passenger, but it didn't help a bit. Working in the cockpit puts you in a different headspace—plus there's the constant company—and so I inevitably came down with a severe case of boredom.

I still remember the video map showing the plane's progress over Europe and then Russia, the plane icon inching over those former Soviet republics. I knew the big names on the map—Lithuania, Latvia, Belarus—but I wanted to know exactly which places we were flying over. The flight computers were encyclopedic and offered a wealth of knowledge, but from where I sat, I felt removed. I missed watching the cities on the map flit past me: Pskov, Smolensk, Tver, Kaluga, Bryansk.

The cloud cover outside my window rarely broke. All I saw was opaque white with an occasional arctic blue or nighttime black of endless infinity. I felt like I was watching one of those experimental art films on endless loop set to a monotonous soundtrack.

The nothingness outside my window and the turbines' whine only added to my malaise. At this point, I was convinced the flight would never end. I'm sure if I'd had company I would've been OK, but there's no way to sugarcoat it: I was lonely.

We made it to Moscow but I still had the layover at Sheremetyevo International and the 3.5 hour leg to Schiphol, followed by the 8.5 hour trip to Bombay, and then the 2.5 hour leg to Kolkata. The six hours on the hard wooden chair at the airport Starbucks was the worst of it, and confirmed my resolve that should I ever be taken hostage by terrorists with itchy trigger fingers for a similar duration, I'd request to be put out of my misery.

• • •

"I'd like you to meet someone, Clay. This is Amar. Amar, meet Clay." Plim looks at me with her soft brown eyes and then to the young man lying motionless on the cot. She kneels at his side, resting a hand on his shoulder.

"Hello. It's nice to meet you," I say hovering over them both.

"Do you remember any of your Marathi, Clay?" Plim says. "Try making your greeting a little more personal."

She holds Amar's bony brown hand in hers and strokes his head, speaking to him in gentle tones. "*Khup divasāt bhetalo nāhi. Su-prabhāt*, Amar?" she says.

Plim's Marathi is better than mine on account of the fact that she actually *speaks* the Maharashtra-state dialect whereas I've stolen some phrases from the web. But I made it here, all decked out in my blue apron and latex gloves like the rest of the volunteers. A red bandana is tied over my mop of graying hair, and the only way I could make this look cool would be if I were a twenty-year-old UC Santa Cruz environmental studies major.

The gloves on my hands feel awkward, but they're the most important item of all because they protect me from disease and infection at the Kolkata hospice. In fact, all the volunteers wear gloves except Plim, who refuses to wear them because...because...*I don't know why she refuses to wear them.* I catch a glimpse of another volunteer and I realize we look like third-world operating room attendants awaiting instruction.

"You want me to make my greeting more personal, Plim? Like this?" I manage a small bow in Amar's direction.

Plim huffs and stage whispers to Amar.

"Clay's a good friend of mine, Amar, and you can trust him. But he's a little awkward at first." She looks at me with sorrow in her eyes.

"*Namaskār?*" I say with a rising tone and smile, bowing again.

"Better, Clay. Except '*namaskār*' means 'hello.' It's not a question, so you don't use an upward inflection when you say it," Plim says.

"*Thū kasā āhes?*" I say, reading off a piece of paper in my pocket. I bow deeply and hope Amar isn't offended by my pronunciation.

"You can stop bowing, Clay. This isn't feudal Japan."

"Hey, I've got an idea. Stop criticizing me! You could actually be supportive instead of picking on me," I say.

Plim huffs and whispers to Amar.

"Someone's feeling sensitive. Don't worry. He's often like this."

"Yeah, that's what everybody says after they hurt your feelings! Let me do my job, and maybe I'll actually learn something."

Plim blows some hair out of her face and sighs. "Fair enough."

"So, where's your wife? I thought she was joining us," I say.

"Change of plans. Randala couldn't make it. Work to do back home."

"Are you kidding? Oh my god. I thought it was going to be the three of us."

"Me too," she says, looking at me with those worried eyes of hers.

I'm still trying to get my bearings on my second day at the West Bengal hospice, and it's taking a lot out of me. Everything is new: the people, language, culture, job. I'm anxious, yes, but Plim's been her wonderful self to ensure I'm comfortable. The Missionaries of Service of Kolkata are the ones who run the hospice, and they've done everything they can to make me feel welcome.

I continue smiling at Amar, not because I'm happy, but because it's the only expression I can feign in light of his grave condition. I press my latex-gloved hand against his hand and look at his face for a reaction, but there's nothing. He doesn't seem to be present, so my cultural bumblings aren't a concern. From what I've heard, he's hanging onto this world by a thread, and it's unlikely he'll last until morning.

The Kalighat Home of the Pure Spirit's volunteers wear the same uniform: shorts, flip-flops, T-shirt, gloves, and a blue apron. Plim and I are inside the men's ward where the walls are alabaster white and brown beams crisscross the ceiling like a ski lodge. But this is no mountain retreat, just a single-room care facility where two dozen patients lie in cots like soldiers in a field hospital. Milky light pours through the arched windows above our heads, warming the interior.

My nose is running from the smell of disinfectant, but my discomfort is trivial compared to what the patients are going through. The acrid smell comes from the constant scrubbing and sanitizing—a grim necessity given the staff's contact with the ill and dying.

The men in the hospice are in various stages of terminal illness, but the staff and volunteers go about their duties with care and efficiency. Death is an hourly occurrence, and we all know this is the last stop for the patients who arrive here.

The Home of the Pure Spirit has a storied history steeped in its founders' vision from over a century ago. The room we're working in is similar to another famous hospice created by Mother Teresa in 1952 to care for the dying. Her Home of the Pure Heart set the standard for hospice care and was the first institution of its kind to embrace the poor so they could die with dignity.

"Hey, look what I found!" I say, holding my gloved hands in the air. "What's this? Oh, they're protective gloves! Now available to every healthcare worker in the world!"

Plim puts a bare hand on Amar's, shoulder then looks at his emaciated body where sores cover his trunk, arms, and legs. His cheeks are sunken like an AIDS patient, and he can't be more than ninety pounds. I'm guessing he's in his early twenties, but his skeletal body reminds me of ghoulish Holocaust photos. His eyes are open but he doesn't speak, instead offering a grunt or groan to suffice for "yes" or "no." But none of this seems to dampen Plim's spirit. She looks at me holding my hands in the air.

"I'm not wearing gloves, Clay. How would you feel if the only hands you felt were covered in latex? Would you know the comfort of human touch?" she says.

"News flash. You can't work if you're dead. The gloves are here so you can stay healthy and keep working," I say.

She lifts Amar's left arm and examines it closely.

"I'm a westerner, Clay. I can buy medication for any condition I catch here. Plus, I'm already healthy."

I sit down next to her and try another tack.

"Forget diarrhea and dysentery. Have you met their friends? Malaria. Hepatitis. HIV. Polio. Typhoid. A third-world hospice isn't the place for carelessness."

"Calling India the third world is a tired stereotype and shows your ignorance. Every westerner thinks India is polluted rivers, bindis, and elephants. Your clichés are as old as the building we're sitting in," she says.

"Take it down a notch, OK? Remember, I'm not the enemy here."

"What if you lived a life without love, Clay? A life without kindness and consideration. Where you struggled daily and only found occasional light."

"I don't have to imagine it."

Plim sighs. "Look, touch is the only thing I can give them, and it *does something* for them. I have nothing else to ease their pain."

"We agree on that." A curtain billows in the corner as a volunteer walks by with hot tea and biscuits. The food is for patients and staff alike, but the patients always eat first because they need the nutrition.

"Amar?" Plim says, trying to stir him. "Wake up. It's time for the moisturizer...Listen to the sound of his name, Clay. *Amar.* It sounds regal, like old Hollywood."

"Like Omar Sharif from *Lawrence of Arabia.*"

"What?" she says.

"*Lawrence of Arabia?*"

Plim stares at me blankly.

"With Omar Sharif and Peter O'Toole?...*I shall be at Aqaba. That is written,*" I say. She continues staring at me. "Nothing?...Never mind." I sigh.

"Forget the movie quotes and focus on what we're doing."

It's impolitic to say it, but this is god's waiting room. The poor's poorest are unable to die dignified deaths in hospitals and nursing homes, and it's not just for lack of money. They'd still be shunned for their caste. No support structures or communities exist to take of them, so they come here and we do the best we can.

Plim lifts Amar's hand and a strand of gray hair falls in front of her face.

"First, you look for signs of infection," she says, instructing me, pulling his left arm into her lap. She rubs moisturizer around his sores and then does the same thing on his other arm. She applies the same compound to his legs. There's a groan from Amar as she rolls him over.

"I'm sorry," she says gently. "This will only take another minute." She finishes with his back and legs and rolls him back over. "I'm done now. You did great." She rests a hand on his heart and looks over at me with those sad brown eyes.

The work we're doing here is important, but I don't say that to compliment myself. It's the other volunteers who deserve the credit—the people who have been here months or years investing their energy to build something meaningful. My appreciation for them grows daily, and they're the reason the Home of the Pure Spirit succeeds in its mission.

Recently, I've become a more active volunteer, taking shifts in the hospice's makeshift morgue—this, in addition to my regular duties on the men's ward floor. Working in the morgue is part of every volunteer's responsibilities, despite how off-putting or macabre it may seem.

Not long after I arrived, Plim and I wrapped a patient's body in ceremonial cloth after he passed. The staff and volunteers held a small religious ceremony in the garden per his culture's custom to honor his memory. We prayed together and alone, and then took his body for burial. I'm not a religious person, but everything about the service was deeply meaningful.

I'm definitely out of my element here, but I'm learning to be OK with my new surroundings and responsibilities. I'm learning that death with dignity is important, especially given the high numbers of Kolkata's poor and the scant options available for the terminally ill.

It's comforting that the Home of the Pure Spirit's mission hasn't changed since its inception over a hundred years ago. It feels good to be a part of its enduring legacy. I feel fortunate to be among the missionaries and volunteers, and I think our work is admirable. We carry the same charge forward the founders did, and I haven't felt this connected to my work in a long time. At night before I fall asleep, I've even found a small peace in my heart that grows stronger every day.

15

EARLIER IN THE DAY IT felt right and Frisbee in the park was cool, except she couldn't throw and mostly just flung the wobbly disc at you as you made small talk. You stopped playing after a minute because there was no joy in the air, no magic, and it felt like she was going through the motions to please you. But, who are you kidding? Your heart wasn't in it either.

She looked lithe and lean in her little cut-offs and tank top, sun-drenched and carefree, padding on the lawn by the softball fields. Her long hair bristled in the wind, raven strands licking the air like a serpent's tongue, and you devoured every curve. Softball players unpacked their gear on diamonds of brown and green, but you hardly noticed.

It was a perfect Sunday in Central Park, a day incapable of being ruined by calls of nature or duty, and your blanket unfurled with a view of the game. The spread you'd planned was good: wine, fruit, cheese, a baguette, seltzer, chocolate. There was some chitchat about the city at this time of year, but her hair was so close and by then it was too late.

"Clay, stop touching my hair. I'm not a pet!" she said.

"But it's so nice."

"I already know about your hair fetish. You said so on the phone."

She arched like a cat to get some food, but you controlled yourself, even with those lips within striking distance. She righted herself, and a small jolt tickled your heart.

"I'm not admitting anything about your thick, lustrous, dark hair," you smiled. She shot you a look as you wriggled into a sitting position for a game view.

"It's dead cells," she said with her back tight against your chest. You cuddled her like a bear and inhaled deeply, hoping she wouldn't notice. There was a magnificent smell and volume, and you stared at the silky strands.

"It's incredibly soft, the epitome of spectacular, the high art of beautiful," you whispered.

"It's dry and I have tons of split ends. I get out of the shower and don't even blow it dry."

"It's magic on earth. I could spend all day lost in its soft darkness," you said.

"Do you and my hair want to be left alone?" She laughed and squeezed your arm and then your lips in an awkward first kiss. "Are you judging me, Clay?"

Yes, you were judging her, but it wasn't to be cruel. It was a first date, after all, and that's what people did: tally a partner's merits on an imaginary scorecard. You liked her personality and intellect, but she was neither buxom nor comely, not that it mattered.

Traditional beauty meant little in your eyes because you were here for something else. It was her hair, smooth skin, and symmetrical features that wowed you, because they meant she could produce strong children. Kids were a mandatory in your book, and you wanted a romantic partner who felt the same. Yes, you'd cast a critical eye on her form, but not because you were cruel—it was an evolutionary mandate, impolitic and impolite.

There was a *plink* on the softball field as bat connected with ball, and people cried out. A line drive sailed over the shortstop's mitt and the runner rounded first, going for more. The runner kept at it as her team's screams propelled her past second until she arrived at third to a round of applause. Her smile grew wide as the whoops from her team filled her with joy.

"It's thick, soft, magical darkness," you said, touching her hair.

"You're easily impressed."

"Only by you."

"Clay, come on. You're creeping me out. It's a first date. You shouldn't come on so strong."

Maybe she'd stem the flow of sadness that saddled your spirit and cuddle you from darkness till dawn. It was ridiculous, you knew, thinking you could turn her from lovable into loving so she'd care for you like you were a small boy.

There was the dip in the small of her back as it curved to her hips, and that you liked. Your eyes traveled from her neck along the ribs of her tank top and past her shorts until you found those thighs, tan like caramel. She rolled onto her stomach and caught you staring again.

"Clay! Stop! You're creeping me out."

"I'm sorry. It's just that I like you." And then you realized your dating faux pas. "I shouldn't have—"

"I think I like you too, despite your creepy dating habits!" She made a face at you. "How long have you been a pilot?" You lay down and pulled her close. She fit like a puzzle piece.

"Awhile."

"A *long* while?" she asked.

"You could say that."

You picked up a handful of hair, smiling brightly, and marveled at the ink-black strands. You watched it spill through your fingers and your joy sank, then grabbed another handful of silk and felt your spirit renewed. You caressed it in your hands and your hope soared.

By now, the sun was low in the sky, and softball players were packing their duffels and backslapping their buds. You had to pee but you held it. You had a turn in the morning, but you ignored it. You packed up together to leave and resolved you wouldn't let the Sunday crazies get to you.

She took your hand as you walked south on Broadway, and you admired the planters brimming with color and the chatty alfresco diners in their sunglasses. Cars clogged the intersection at W 73rd Street, and Trader Joe's was up ahead, its towering edifice casting a shadow across the street.

"Do you need any groceries? Is there anything you need before you go home?" she said. There was no desperation in her voice, she wanted you to be prepared for the week ahead.

"Nah, I'm good." You smiled, and she hugged you in a polite goodbye and gave you a small peck.

The train stairs were only a dozen yards away, and the black headphone cord from your phone was unraveled as you turned away.

"Are you hungry? I could make you a snack." You turned around and her face said *concern* and her voice was matter-of-fact. "I have stuff for sandwiches. Something to eat."

Is this it? you wondered to yourself. It was date number one, and you hadn't even pulled any of the moves HazMatt taught you. I mean, sure, you were horny, but you'd made a pact with yourself to follow a dating plan.

You'd start slow and build something with a new woman, taking her out for a few months and getting to know her. Picnics and bike rides might lead to dinners and concerts. God knows, you wanted a girlfriend. Trips to the Hamptons and Hudson Valley could lead to the Poconos and Hunter Mountain.

You'd canoodle with her at The Strand, lingering at the fiction tables like a couple of NYU kids, trading looks as you browsed the new releases. You'd let your baritone do the work, exhaling warmth on her skin as you read book blurbs in funny voices. The store's floorboards would creak underfoot and float your hope that you'd finally found a cute book reader.

But your dating plan meant a dramatic change of course, and that was the hardest part. From now on, you'd say no to the party girls and nighttime haunts and the late night texts that said WHAT R U UP TO? You'd resist the libidinous temptations of dimly lit wine bars and any place where a bare thigh in a short dress might invite a lingering caress. You'd ignore the plunging necklines, soft lips, and the rhapsody of scented perfume.

But now, you were headed to her house.

• • •

The elevator doors close behind you and she turns left, so you follow her like a dog on a leash as she heads down the hallway. She arrives at her front door, does a little two-step, then looks you in the eye.

"It's nothing special," she says.

"Don't say that."

"Really. I have the smallest studio apartment in the city. I'm sure of it."

"I highly doubt it."

That's what comes out of your mouth, but it's not what you want to say. What you want to say is, *You're beautiful and smart with a great job and a ton of friends and I didn't think I'd have a chance in hell with a girl like you. My gums are receding and my time on earth is probably half over. What could you possibly see in me?*

Somehow you suppress the urge to monologue, and her brown eyes catch yours. The look isn't come-hither, but it's not chaste either, so you swallow and imagine the possibilities. You find her lips soft and pink like watermelon bubble gum.

"Come in," she says, opening the door.

The walls are as white as copy paper and the furnishings sparse, with an L-shaped couch in the room's center and a bed off to the side. You move toward the window while she busies herself in the kitchen.

"You want something to drink?"

"Sure. Water. Thanks."

The backpack slides off your sweaty shoulders and sloughs to the floor. You feel the A/C on your skin. Residential towers rise in every direction before your face, and you feel the thousands of eyes upon you. There's a small swath of Central Park visible between buildings, with maples bushy and green and a few Kwanzan cherry trees.

You flop on the couch and stretch out, finding no paintings or photos to admire, and scant knickknacks or bric-a-brac on the shelves. The only personal touch is a few multicolored throw pillows lying on the bed.

She's got promise, you think, and you applaud yourself for screening her because you don't think she's unstable or addicted. You don't see her as a boozer or druggie, liar or manipulator—and her career seems sorted out, too. But she's not perfect, and that's important, because you want someone real with issues of their own. Who wants to be with someone perfect? You feel hopeful sitting here with thoughts of something meaningful and long-lasting.

Of course, you hope she's here for the right reasons and that she wants the same things. Most importantly, you hope that this won't fizzle out like so many of your online dates. You wouldn't mind having sex, but that's her decision, not yours. Still, sex soothes because it takes away life's pain like daily masturbation.

She sits down with drinks in hand, and you talk quietly, caressing her hair and touching her shoulders. You caress her arms and legs and take her mouth in yours. You're kissing her slowly, but she soon overpowers and then mounts you. Your hands move to her chest, waist, and hips, and she arches her back and moans. She's panting and grinding into your hand, and then she gives you a look.

Alone with her now, your mind wanders to what she's into. You want to try something new...another position, maybe? The current setup isn't bad, but dry humping comes in last on your carnal to-do list. But it doesn't take long for the temperature to climb, so you go a little aggro to see what she's into.

You shove her face into the couch cushions, pressing your hips in her ass with lips wet on her neck and a fistful of hair tight in your hand. She's totally at your mercy, bent like an acrobat, and gasping like she's drowning on land. *Shit.*

"Oh my god! Are you OK?"

"I hyperventilate when I'm turned on," she says.

She kisses you deeply and returns, face down, to the couch, and you're kissing her everywhere and feeling her up like a teenager. Her lovely ass is in your crotch, but her breaths are still labored and her eyes flit up into her head, then disappear. So you stop again.

"You sure you're OK?"

She nods.

Her face morphs into a kaleidoscope of pleasure as you stroke her thighs. You're touching her everywhere at once because you've got a shot at some you-know-what. But you didn't plan any of this. You only have one condom and a half tab of linty Viagra floating around in your backpack. You have no idea how to build on this—more importantly, does she want more?

A sharp punch lands on your face and you wince, disoriented, and wait for a rebuke. But there's no pain or lecture because it's all in your head and nothing's really happened. Her hands are beneath her, nowhere in sight, so you push away the image and stop what you're doing.

"Are you OK, Clay?"

You nod.

You look her in the eyes and caress her to make sure this journey is consensual, so you ask again if she's all right. She nods and kisses you back. You move her onto her back and work your hand up and inside and watch her chest rise, head sinking into the cushions with her neck exposed. She's warm like sunshine and wet like a sponge, and you take off her shirt and bra. *I wonder if I should be doing this. Maybe I should wait.*

You move her hands to the front of your shorts and there's a slap across your face. You wince and flinch, but it's not her because her hands are in yours. Now, something's in your mouth and you don't want it there so you shake your head and pull off her shorts to find her bushy and beautiful.

"I'm hot."

"Let me turn up the A/C," she says.

She moves to the controls by the window and you get an eyeful of caramel skin. She's short, yes, but well proportioned and beautiful for thirty-three. Plus, let's face it, everything you like is present and accounted for. Seeing her hair cascade halfway down her back is beyond erotic and sends a shockwave through your libido.

You get up, meet her by the window, and take her back to bed. Now that she's in your mouth, you're sated until you feel another uncomfortable sensation and your desire flags. You collapse in a heap with your eyes shut tight.

"What's wrong?" she says.

"I'm good. Really, I'm good. Just tired."

You wipe away the moisture in your eyes and return to her neck, avoiding her gaze. She's hyperventilating before long and you return to her lips, warm and wet, until the pain subsides.

"I have to pee," she says.

The bathroom door clicks closed and you play with yourself to see if you can raise the flag, but there's nothing. You get up to fish out the boner pill from the depths of your pack, then zip back to bed. The toilet flushes and bathroom sink runs as you gobble the pill to shore up your confidence.

You reach firmness before you know it and don the condom, but by then, you're impatient and have no desire for more foreplay. You ask her if it's OK to proceed and she nods, so you enter her and she winces. You knew she wasn't ready, but your impulse got the best of you—even if your brain liked seeing her hurt a little. If she'll suffer for you, maybe she could love you, too.

You tried making up for your mistake and slowed your lovemaking because you didn't want her to think you were the asshole. It was your way of saying you were a good person, even if you didn't always do the right thing.

But then a switch flicks and you think to yourself: *She's going to think I'm a namby-pamby. A poof. A girly man. Especially if I keep up with this sensitive shit.* And with that, the whole tender lovemaking vanishes and you take her.

You're in sync, together. She looks you in the eye and you feel it. It's going to be good this time, because you know your destination and she's along for the ride. But then it happens, her eyes flutter and the whites of her eyes appear. She disappears into a fugue state and she's gone.

This weird feeling overcomes you and something sick flashes before your eyes, and in that instant you realize she's been abused. She's done this disappearing act before, you reason, and learned how to protect the fragile girl within.

You finish loudly in her and your orgasm is off the charts, like you've burst a blood vessel. The climb is so high and the fall so perfect that you feel cuddled in a cloud—such a brilliant little death. She looks so beautiful in your arms, so vulnerable, and you caress her face and consider her lovingly. She's done everything you asked and yet you're filled with shame.

But the look on her face isn't anger or fear—or hurt. She's not mad at you, not at all, because her eyes are fixed on an invisible plane beyond your right shoulder. You look down at her and call her name and she doesn't respond. You caress her and she doesn't move. A pit rises in your stomach, because she's not here.

16

SHE IS SUCH THE WHOLE PACKAGE, WITH
SMOOTH SKIN, SLENDER BODY, AND SWEET
PERSONALITY. SHE IS GIVING AND LOVING AND
YOU WILL ENJOY THE SWING OF HER SEXY HIPS.
THE LOOK IN HER BEAUTIFUL EYES MIGHT TURN
YOU ON TO LEVELS YOU COULD NOT DREAM OF.
SHE WILL DELIGHT YOU. ALIENA. 27 YEARS OLD.
5'7", 115 LBS, 34C-26-34.

THEIR PHONE NUMBER IS ON the screen, but for now you ignore it, browsing through the picture gallery like the horny man you are. You click on another thumbnail photo and try to ignore your conflicting feelings of shame and desire.

You swore you wouldn't return, and yet here you are again, with the bevy of beauties on your screen and your credit card in hand. You're ashamed to admit the service occupies a permanent space on your phone, camouflaged as a benign contact to obscure the nature of its offerings.

Your desire grows strongest when you're hungry or lonely or scared or tired and in need of comfort. This is your go-to on nights and weekends when you find yourself downroute and craving the heat of female flesh.

And now the phone is tight against your cheek, and you hope the throbbing will stop, the thick peanut butter buzz of discomfort that makes your saliva thick and your head hurt. But this isn't an addict's anticipation, just a background of sadness like a personal dark cloud.

The greasy glass slips between your ear and cheek, the number rings, and you feel your anxiety tick up a notch. But there's no reason to worry, because you're only a credit card to them. They get paid when you get laid, so you'll play your role on the phone and they'll play theirs until the deed is done. And now there's a voice in your ear.

"Entertainment. Yes?"

"Uh...Hi."

"Credit card number and expiration."

"I'm looking for um...I'd like to..."

"Credit card number and driver's license required. Verification first time," the man says.

You click on another photo and the full size image doesn't disappoint, the brunette has silky brown hair falling down her back and a pretty smile. The mouse clicks and the photo grows larger so you can get a better angle on her form.

"I'm on file. My card number is 4521...2955...5458–"

"3711 36th Street #10D?"

"Yes, yes."

"What may we be assistance?"

"Who is available ton–"

"Eastern girls many tonight available. Polish. Hungarian. Romanian. Czech. Serbian girl, nice? Traci, Danya, Anasatasia, Yana, Zlata, Veronika. All we have."

"How much?"

There's another woman on your screen you like more, posing in a series of lifestyle shots, sweet not sexy. In one photo, she's lounging at a dinette, considering the camera with loving eyes and a meal made for two like a young bride making a new home. In another, she's cozy by a fireplace in a skirt and heels holding a glass of wine. You imagine coming home to her for conversation and comfort, maybe more.

SHE IS A DIVINE SOUL AND HER HANDS WILL MASSAGE YOU AND TAKE AWAY ALL OF THE WORRY. SHE WILL ROMANCE YOU ALL NIGHT LONG UNTIL YOU ACHIEVE THE ULTIMATE STRESS RELEASE. YULIA. 29 YEARS OLD. 5'6". 110 LBS. 34D-29-32.

"Ayam, Leita, Koelle, Finsesh, Salya. All good very excellent, my friend. You like young or over thirty? Blonde and brunette, green and brown eyes. Tonight available. Who for tonight you like?"

"Brunette with green eyes, yes."

"$350 one hour. $600 two hours."

"I want two hours. Yulia seems nice."

"Yes, yes. Taste very good, but Yulia not available sorry."

You click on another profile. "Aliena?"

"Taste very good and not available sorry. Kendin, Marulia, Roen, Milkona, Pralsish we have. Meena very nice new girl for you. Very sweet Meena. Good heart. Thirty-one years old. Brunette and green eyes. Very nice sweet girl Meena. Good smile. Thin and very pretty. Short wait for busy you, my friend. I send a car for her now?"

"Does she speak English?"

"She has a good heart and you'll relax fully, I promise for her."

"Yes, but does she speak English?"

"Meena, yes. English excellent. Security code on back of credit card."

"4-2-9." But you're still clicking on profiles and looking at women when you land on a gallery of a blonde dressed like a comely astronaut in silver lamé. She's wearing firecracker-red lipstick, a mini-skirt, push-up bra, and heels, posing on a moonscape set with a toy phaser and pouting for the camera.

ARE YOU THE PROFESSOR? LET HER BE YOUR BEST STUDENT. THIS COLLEGE GIRL WANTS TO GO TO THE MOON SOME DAY. LET HER STRADDLE YOUR ROCKET SHIP AS YOU LAUNCH INTO SPACE. YOU WILL DELIGHT IN HER ALMOND SKIN AND GREEN EYES AND SHE WILL ACCOMPANY YOU TO NEW HEIGHTS. 30 YEARS OLD. MILANA. 5'9". 130 LBS. 34C-25-26.

"The charge on your credit card will be from Pestrova Enterprises."

"Wait. Is Milana available?"

"Taste excellent, but not available. Sorry. Meena available."

"Yes, Meena. OK. How long?"

"The driver will pick her up now and we are short wait for you my busy friend. Very close is she to you. Your time will be lovely, two hours and goodnight thank you."

• • •

You find the keys in the prescription bottle in the junk drawer and drag the fire safe to the couch to check the contents. The lid opens and you find the package covered in bubble wrap, bulbous around its form. The piece looks dirty, judging by the brown flakes that have settled at the package's bottom, and you handle it gently, because it's loaded.

Outside the window, a man in the apartment building across the way is playing a game of fetch with a tennis ball and dog on the building's roof. He throws the ball and the dog races along the rooftop at top speed until it skitters to a stop inches from the edge, grabbing the ball in its mouth. Watching this scene puts you in a state of high anxiety, and you wince every time the ball leaves the man's hands, fearing the ball will tumble over the edge and the dog along with it. You stand at the window, a part of you wanting to yell across the way and ask the man what the fuck he thinks he's doing.

You look down at your windowsill and find that the plants, once thriving, are now brown from weeks of neglect. The snake plant's vibrant leaves are curled like a dead man's hand, and the fern is listless and dry.

The box cutter slices away the bubble wrap to reveal some burnishing on the gun, a reminder of its previous life. The piece is heavy in your hands and you think back to the teen on the playground and Sam saving you from your fate. You think back to being robbed by Scuzzbucket and the cities on the map of your endless drives around Southern California: Morongo Valley, Yucca Valley, Joshua Tree.

You eject the magazine. It drops into your palm and you rack the slide to extract the cartridge from the chamber. The bullet lands on the table and you push the rounds from the magazine, counting them out: *1, 2, 3, 4, 5...*

You point the gun at your head, but not because you're sad or thinking about the events of the past. In fact, the abuse and lies are only footnotes to your story. What hurts isn't the grief over the past, but the life you've led since, drowning in sex and lies that only add to your sorrow.

The adorable twentysomethings in your neighborhood fill you with jealousy, not joy, because they've nourished bonds of support and can lean on someone when they need a friend. There's probably someone they can list as an EMERGENCY CONTACT on a medical form, or somewhere they can go when they feel weary.

You're not sad or depressed because there's no room for sorrow when you've got so much rage. You burned every bridge and neglected to pave your roads, and all of it's come back to haunt you. And here you sit, the mayor of a city with a population of one.

You have such a nice family, you said to the father of four on the Q train last week. The fiftysomething man was middle-aged handsome with tufts of gray hair and broad shoulders with an angel wife and four girls—blondes all of them. The littlest was around four, and the family was laughing and holding onto the grab bars on the rollicking subway car. They laughed as the train lumbered along, and you imagined what it would've been like to grow up with love.

You cock the hammer with a flick of your thumb and point the gun at your temple in the classic suicide position. And then you switch positions and open wide, sticking the pistol inside your mouth and gagging at the taste of steel on your tongue. You pull the trigger. *Click.*

Now the gun is back at your head, and you feel your rage build like DeNiro in the Russian roulette scene in *Deer Hunter.* You imagine yourself the Vietnam prisoner of war and make the same crazed expression he does before he explodes. And you don't have to search for emotion as you audition your suicide, because the hate simmers like a pot before the boil.

And now you're playing up the emotions like you're starring in your own suicide movie, channeling DeNiro from the film. Your face morphs into a myriad of expressions as you search for the right combination of scared as fuck, brave as hell, and terrified beyond compare. You squeeze your eyes tight and pull the trigger. *Click.*

There's a dull thud on the couch as the gun falls to the cushions and now you're lying on your side, angry and alone—too afraid to die and too scared to live.

And now, there's a buzz at the intercom of your apartment because the girl you ordered is here.

17

THE CHIGASAKI ROLLS INTO THE parking lot with its engine humming. I realize I'm the day's first visitor, so I park by the trailhead and kill the engine. The kickstand flips out and sinks into the dirt, and I take in the vista of oaks and elms and take a breath of fresh air. The air is cool, and the trail's entrance is covered in leafy branches like an archway.

The texts and tweets can wait, so I stash my phone in the bike's locked compartment and pull off my helmet. The breeze cools my skin as the backpack sloughs onto the bike's saddle and I check the contents. I have my water, book, and a snack, but the most important items are in my fleece: the cigar and lighter.

The ground crunches underfoot as I hike up the incline, but the effort is no workout, and soon I'll be on the ridge's top and able to enjoy the preserve's charms. The leaves are dewy from the night before, and I occasionally have to pin back a wet tree branch as my feet clomp along the trail. I move higher and fidget with the cigar, rolling it between my fingers and thumb.

After twenty minutes, I arrive at the switchbacks and start up the path with no flag in enthusiasm, looking back to the parking lot to check my progress. I retrieve the cigar as I navigate the serpentine path and look again to see how far I've come. My bike is obscured by the horizon, and the gray morning awaits the sun's entrance through the clouds.

The lighter snaps on, baking the cigar's end in preparation. "Toasting" is a pre-smoking ritual where the cigar's end is burned with a quick back and forth sweep of the lighter. It's a necessity for cigar smokers because it helps the cigar maintain an even burn once lit.

Just to be clear, I'm not one of *those* cigar smokers—you know, the loud and obnoxious types who huddle outside bars with booming voices that carry blocks at a time. I've never been a group smoker, and I shun cigar circles because I like the solitude of solo smokes. But my avocation as cigar smoker has been a challenge, because it's excluded me from most places and made finding anywhere to smoke a real challenge.

As a rule, we cigar smokers don't puff at home because it stinks up our abodes, and we don't smoke in public anymore because it's illegal. Bars and restaurants used to welcome us, but that was before the great shaming of smoking, back when Wham! ruled the airwaves.

But in Queens I've found a few smoking havens among the preserves and trails that sit on the borough's outskirts. In fact, Queens is home to a bevy of trails that are seldom used because they have no Wi-Fi or vanilla lattes to soothe the boredom of city dwellers.

My new favorite hiking spot is Bandera Preserve, a one-and-a-half-mile loop that wends up a slope and series of switchbacks and levels off on a flat trail. It's a short walk that terminates in a cul-de-sac in a field of grass with a rock wall where I can sit and smoke and watch climbers perform their feats of derring-do.

There's one way in and out of Bandera Preserve, which makes the hike intimate and lets me enjoy my cigar in the quietest of spaces. Trees and grass are everywhere, so I'm mindful not to start a conflagration in the small forest because, well, that would be bad. And yes, I'm a smoking scofflaw—smoking isn't allowed here, but the hikers I've seen haven't raised a fuss.

There's the sound of leaves crunching on the footpath, and I swivel to see a flash of blonde hair bobbing between the trees. The ground's vibration tells me I have more company, and I notice the blonde is part of a trio making their way up the trail behind me. I don't recall seeing anyone when I started out, so the sight is odd, but no less welcome given the day's promise.

I squint in an effort to make out anything else in the hiking party and find another woman and man with the blonde, but none are dressed for a day in the sun. In fact, they're wearing long pants and shirts with heavy boots on a day that promises eighty-degree temps. There's considerable clomping on the path, and I see that the group is carrying large cans that scrape the ground and make a noise every time they hit a trail rock. A *klong* rings out across the ridgeline every few minutes like a clock tower sounding the hour.

My quads carry me up the switchbacks, and there's a eucalyptus grove on the ridgeline with bark peeling from the trunks like pencil shavings. It's been a dry summer and the trees are sloughing off bark as they reach higher.

My sneakers kick up dust as I lope along in my shorts and T-shirt. I can already feel the sun's warmth on my skin, teasing the day's heat. The cigar rises to my mouth, and I light the business end, the flame licking it like a tongue. I puff and puff in great draws to create an ember as bright as a sun. It's been a horrific few months with all that's happened, and I spent a little more than I should have on the Dominican robusto because I wanted to spoil myself—I deserve it.

I look down the switchbacks and find the trio continuing their ascent but not paying me much attention. After fifteen minutes, I arrive at the summit and see the trail's end a couple of hundred yards away, terminating in the grassy cul-de-sac and rock wall.

"Hello!? Hello!?"

The man in the hiking party is trying to get someone's attention, so I turn back and look out of curiosity. The group is thirty or so yards away. My eyes examine his face and those of his companions before I continue on.

"Hello!? Hello!? Excuse me!" he says in a British accent. I look over my shoulder again with a puff of smoke as I exhale.

"Are you talking to me!?"

"Captain Sonnering, it's good to see you!"

I stop and pivot around, checking his face and frame to see if there's anything that might spark my recognition—but there's nothing.

"Do I know you?"

"Captain Clay Sonnering? Born in Princeton, New Jersey in 1972. RASH Airlines pilot since 1998. 3711 36th Street in New York. Apartment 10D?" My face scrunches but I still don't know who he is.

"Is this a joke or do I know you?"

"It's very cold out, Captain. You could catch a chill out here."

"This must be some sort of joke HazMatt put you up to! Ha-ha! Very funny. Tell him the jig's up and leave me in peace." I turn and continue hiking.

"It's quite cold out, Captain. Bloody freezing, actually," the man says turning to the brunette in his group. "Wouldn't you say so?" he says to her.

"Quite right! It's monkeys outside!" the young woman says.

"See, it's not just me, Captain. Really, you ought to warm up or you could become...*deathly ill*," he says.

"Look, leave me alone! Tell HazMatt his joke is...You know what? Nevermind!" I'm only a hundred yards from the grass field at the cul-de-sac's end.

"Captain, please! I beg of you. Please warm up now so you don't get sick!"

"Leave me alone!"

"A fire. Yes! That's what you need. A nice crackling fire to keep you toasty and warm."

I'm moving faster toward the rock wall, puffing nervously, glancing over my shoulder every few seconds to make sure they're not gaining on me. Over my shoulder, there's the sound of water pouring like someone taking a hose to a flower bed.

I turn to find the blonde and brunette walking among the scrub brush, pouring their cans' contents onto the grass and bushes near the eucalyptus grove. They return to the dirt path and the blonde lights a cigarette, flicking it into the dry undergrowth—but nothing happens.

"Shit! Are you insane?! What the hell are you doing?!" I say.

The blonde bends down to the ground and holds her lighter's flame to a pile of dead leaves. There's a whooshing sound and the pile instantly catches fire, smoke drifting across the trail.

"You're insane! This is dry brush! You asshole!"

"Ah...that's better, Captain. *Warmth*. I feel much better, now. This ought to keep you hot enough."

A crackling sound is in the air as the smoke turns to flames that grow around the trio, licking the trail's edge. Their faces are the picture of calm as they block the path back to the parking lot and set their gazes on me. The man produces a handgun and holds it at his side.

"Captain Sonnering, a word from a friend. Don't stick your nose where it doesn't belong," the man says.

"What the hell!? You and I will die up here!" I say.

"You're right about one of those things."

A tree between us goes up like a matchstick as it's consumed by flame, branches burning quickly and searing me in a wall of heat. I twist backward, holding up my hands in an effort to protect myself from the small inferno. The fire spreads quickly along the ridge but the trio remain safe, if only for the moment. My head swivels toward the grass and rock wall behind me, and I realize I'm trapped in the middle with nowhere to go.

The man continues staring at me through the smoke and flames, and my expression changes. *Shit*.

"You're the guy in the video! You run Swoosh Airlines! You fucking asshole!" I try staring at him through the flames, but have to shield my eyes from the bright wall of heat.

"To the death of RASH Airlines—and your own, Captain!" he says. "Enjoy your hike, and don't catch a chill!" The trio disappear behind the inferno and the fire leaps across the trail, joining both sides in flame and making egress impossible.

"Motherfucker!"

"Oh, and Captain? Your friend Plim? The old woman? She screamed like a bitch when we killed her...Enjoy your day!"

Goose bumps run down my arms at the sound of her name, but there's no time to think, except for: *What the hell do I do now?!* I look to the grass field that marks the trail's end and realize there's no escape at the rock wall. I can't climb the vertical face and there's no way to run back to the parking lot. *Is there anything in my backpack?*

I bolt for the grass field at full tilt in hopes of gaining another minute on the flames and find the grass parched and brown from another dry season. The fragile stalks sway in the breeze and I realize the field will go up like tinder once the fire arrives. My cigar drops to the ground and I open my backpack to gulp some water. *Shit, shit, SHIT!*

The fire crackles behind me with the furnace growing closer, and I realize I'm either going to die here or *I'm going to die here.* The grass will go up in seconds once it's consumed but it's...it's...it's already on fire! *The field is on fire!?*

The grass burns brightly in front of me as flames spread through the parcel, sending an acrid plume of smoke in my direction. I slump over coughing and grab my knees, and notice the cigar at my feet is the ignition source. The grass is fully involved and I'm trapped between *two* fires, standing in the only safe zone, a path no wider than a vending machine. The fires roar on both sides of me, searing my skin.

I wait for the movie to start, the tasteful vignette of still images of my life set to a pop soundtrack. But my life doesn't flash before my eyes and there's no sequence of happy childhood images narrated by an earnest vocalist. No one is holding my hand on the first day of school. No birthday party smiling faces. No beach trips. No lemonade stands. No ice cream trucks. Nothing. And now I feel my skin slowly burning as the inferno scorches my back. *Fuck, fuck, FUCK!*

My hair catches fire and I scream, then pound my head like a drum to put it out. And that's when I see the field in front of me isn't on fire any more. The field is a smoldering scar of black ash because it's been consumed by flame and is no longer combustible.

I run through the ashy muck as fast as I can and feel the heat melting my running shoes. I arrive at the field's center, then drop to my knees and assume the crash position as the fire wind roars overhead. I'm gagging and choking, struggling for air as my lungs inhale smoke and soot. My eyes clamp shut and I pray, but to what or whom I don't know. *I'm scared. I'm scared. I don't want to die. I'm scared.*

18

"THE SARIN WILL DISABLE THE close protection detail within thirty seconds and bring death within minutes—unless they get the antidote. There's one dose to revive the Secretary, but everyone else will be...less fortunate," Katrina whispered.

Katrina and Petrova were back at the Times Square hotel in their respective wigs, dining in the lobby's café. On a low table in front of them sat an assortment of baked goods, fruit, and coffee. Katrina reached for her espresso, then touched Petrova lightly on the arm and laughed like a school girl.

By all appearances, the women had spent the morning shopping and were recharging their batteries before heading out again. A half dozen bags brimming with colored tissue and upscale logos sat at their feet as they dined. In the lobby's center, a large vase sat on a wooden pedestal with an exotic arrangement of branches, orchids, and lilies. Guest services was busy with customers, and the open atrium teemed with security.

Katrina touched Petrova again, triggering another bout of laughter as the two eyed the agents at the elevator bank.

"The Secretary will come downstairs, and that's when we start the hydrolysis," Katrina said.

"I'm a little scared, love," Petrova said.

"It's all planned out, so don't worry. Watch the elevators and put your trust in the respirator. The close protection team will stir once the Secretary's in motion."

"How do you know he's going to walk through the lobby, love?"

"He has to in order to get to the motorcade." Katrina didn't need to add *unless he uses a fire exit*. It wasn't always best to articulate every thought on one's mind.

Petrova uncrossed her legs, and her foot slipped and struck a shopping bag, hard. There was a metallic *clank* as the shoe hit an oxygen canister, and the women looked around nervously. The bags held the quick-don masks with hoses connected to oxygen cylinders so they could breathe when the nerve agent was released. And now Petrova's phone was in her face.

"Loss of consciousness. Euphoria. Eye pain. Migraine. Sweating. Drooling. Diarrhea. Confusion. Drowsiness...*Crikey*."

"Are you a nutter? Put that away! Let's move to the coffee bar for a better view," Katrina said. They picked up their bags and stood at the coffee bar as agents stirred by the elevators. "It's show time."

"Let's do it."

"Another espresso, please," Katrina said to the barista, then turned to her comrade. "Put the paper bag on the ground and take out your umbrella."

Petrova did as she was told. A decorative paper bag covered in flowers now sat on the ground next to her. The shopping bag held two plastic sandwich bags, tightly sealed and filled to the brim with liquid. One bag contained water and the other held the nerve agent sarin minus a key molecule. Puncturing the bags would join the two liquids together and give the sarin an additional hydrogen ion so it could release its invisible cloud of toxic gas.

The divider separating the bags was removed and the sandwich bags slumped together like two water balloons. The tip of Petrova's umbrella hovered over the shopping bag. She gripped the handle tightly.

"Get ready."

"I'm on it. When do we put on the masks?"

"Watch for my signal," Katrina said.

Two children raced by the coffee bar in a spirited game of "*You're it!...No, you're it!*" while the women defended the area by their stools like soccer goalies during a cup final. Agents had formed an outward-facing semi-circle by the elevators, and a chime rang out across the lobby. An elevator opened to reveal the Secretary of Defense with several aides and Secret Service in tow.

"Now," Katrina whispered. "The mask. Put it on and break the bags. Break them. Now!"

The masks were tight on their faces, and there was an unsettling *fwoomp!* sound as they sealed tight and a *thhhk!* that confirmed oxygen was flowing. Petrova stabbed the bags furiously with the umbrella like a psycho killer in a teen summer camp horror flick. Liquid pooled at the women's feet as lobby patrons grabbed their throats and coughed in fits.

"I can't breathe," Petrova said.

"You're fine. Stay calm. If you're alive, the mask is working." Katrina smiled at the young Hillingdon girl through her clear plastic face mask and caught a smirk in return. "See, you're OK."

"Kat, really. I can't breathe. My chest hurts." Petrova was coughing and her face looked worried.

"Relax and breathe. I'm having some pain, too, but see? I'm OK. Let's get to the Secretary with the antidote! Come on!" The women rose from their stools and headed toward the close protection detail, which was already under siege by the toxin.

But the Secret Service had already noticed the duo in their respirators across the lobby and had ordered an immediate extraction. A radio alert had been sent to all team members, who had encircled the Secretary and were ushering him to the exit. The women clipped the oxygen canisters to their belts and headed for the Secretary as agents in his detail were overcome and fell like soldiers on a battlefield.

Indeed, all of the Secretary of Defense's entourage, including the man himself, were disabled, as were the majority of hotel staff and visitors who were either bent over rubbing their eyes and vomiting or already passed out. Petrova stepped over a few bodies and approached the Secretary, who was lying face down. She bent over him and stabbed him with the needle, then depressed the plunger in hopes of saving his life. She and Katrina then dragged him to the service entrance where they awaited Sumito, who would ferry them to the safe house.

Petrova was confident, even cocksure, in the midst of her first real field test, and she strutted around the lobby feeling proud. The elder and more experienced Katrina would now see how well the Hillingdon girl could perform under pressure. There was a choking sound and Petrova looked up to find Katrina gasping in her respirator with spittle blanketing the face mask and sweat running down her face.

"Take it off!" Katrina screamed pulling on her face mask and Petrova quickly embraced her comrade in a hug to keep her hands at her sides. "No! Seriously! Get this thing off me! I'm choking!" Katrina head-butted the young girl in an effort to break free but Petrova held on to prevent Katrina from doing anything rash.

"You'll die if you take it off," Petrova said. To their left, two Secret Service agents approached, then immediately stumbled and retched onto the ground. They fell into a pool of their own vomit and soiled themselves.

"Let go! Can't breathe. Can't–"

Petrova's eyes went to Katrina's now foggy face mask and the tube that connected the respirator to the oxygen. It was there on Katrina's rubber lifeline that Petrova noticed a large three-inch-long cut in the oxygen hose. Katrina wasn't breathing in 100% oxygen, but was inhaling poison that filled her bloodstream and drowned her lungs.

"Pet, I can't breathe!" Katrina was heavy in Petrova's arms, but Petrova held on tightly as they stood by the service entrance waiting for Sumito.

A bellhop who'd just arrived on shift discovered the lobby scene. He quickly ran to the double doors and pushed them open. The lobby was being flooded with fresh air and he screamed, "Get out! Everyone get out! It's a gas attack!" People were yelling and running for the street as others came back inside to grab victims and shuttle them out to safety.

Petrova was overcome with nausea, and her eyes were watering as she held Katrina in her arms. The young Hillingdon girl felt a tug on her own rubber lifeline and adjusted the hose as it snaked away from her face to her oxygen tank. She moved the hose out of her way and felt something odd to her fingers. The length of hose came to her face and she examined each inch of it as her eyes scanned its length. And there, along its rubber ridges, she found a cut in her lifeline identical to the one that marred Katrina's equipment.

The women were knocked to the ground as two wobbly Secret Service agents stood over them with P229's aimed at their faces. Their guns were trained on the women, the men using undershirts over their faces like masks to give them a modicum of protection. Petrova looked over to find Katrina lying unconscious in a pool of vomit.

Petrova took in the ongoing panic in lobby scene amid the raised voices as the noise of sirens outside grew closer. People were running about, and Petrova took off her mask. There was a faraway look in her eyes as more armed law enforcement flooded the lobby. She was remarkably calm inside and deliberately increased her respiration, taking in huge gulps of air before exhaling fully, like a prize fighter before a match. There was a sharp pain in her forehead, and blood poured from her nose on to the ground. She grew faint as she hyperventilated and watched as the Secretary was whisked from the lobby with a needle dangling from his arm—and she watched as she then fell to the floor.

19

THE FRONT DOOR WAS PART of the home's charm, and an occasional subject of talk because its pine planks soared over twenty feet to the roofline. The door's grandeur was such that every visitor commented on its size. You couldn't even reach the top with a ladder.

As a child, you fantasized about climbing its face like a free soloist, using its nubs for support as you attempted a summit. The original homebuilders were architects, you knew, and their goal was to fashion a door as dramatic as the home itself.

Why did you come to Princeton, and what was it you hoped to gain? You drove all those miles without so much as a phone call to tell her of your plan, and now you're here in New Jersey—home.

The front door of your childhood home has known you nearly as long as your mom, dad, and brother. The door may even know you *better* than them, if you could say such a thing about an inanimate object. The door saw you off to your first day of school and welcomed you home after songs and story time. It sent you off to graduations at middle school and high school and watched you drive off in your very first car, and it was there the day you left and never returned.

The door saw your fashion mistakes and faux pas, but never judged, staying quiet during your polyester, corduroy, silk, leather, and mullet phases. It looked askance when you came home drunk or stoned, angry or horny, but still said nothing.

You greeted the door thousands of times, fumbling with keys in the dark, in all of your personae: hipster, scenester, wonk, doofus, intellectual, and nerd. The door saw you fat and thin, happy and sad, and always withheld judgment like a good friend.

And now, standing face to face with the edifice, the giant brown door looks faded, like a chocolate bar that's grown chalky with age. But you made it here and it's decision time. *Will you or won't you knock?* Are you going to climb back into your car like a big baby*? It's just a fucking door.*

Your grandmother passed over this threshold on visits short and long. You remember her as the loving matriarch, the one whose company you sought when you needed softness and concern. She loved you and on that count you're certain, and wish you could channel her now in your time of need. But she's long gone and her story's been told, only few will remember her even in memory. Ditto your grandfather, the clan's eclectic character and connoisseur of cigars, jazz music, and all things Count Basie. The only grandparents you ever knew now live on only in memory.

Your brother and his husband passed through this door hundreds of times. You remember him and the home he shared with his "friend" back when you were an adolescent. You remember walking around their place and happening upon their bedroom, where you noticed one large bed.

Your eyes found your brother, and you asked, "Why do you guys only have one bed?"

Your brother smiled and replied without hesitation, "My friend sleeps when I'm at work, and I sleep when he's at work."

"Oh," you said, and that settled everything in your young mind.

You remember your brother and his husband laughing, smoking, and making comments silly and snarky—but mostly how deeply they cared about you. They had so many friends and were loved so much, and yet their story is also over. Can their love from the grave sustain you now?

So many relatives and friends welcomed here are now gone, and you wonder how long until you move on to that other place. You doubt there will be a memo beforehand giving you notice, but somehow you're OK with the specter of death. Celebrity deaths and famous funerals are ironically invigorating because they remind you of the value of your days.

There's actually some comfort at being here and knowing the door will carry on with its duties after you pass on. The front door will log another generation's secrets and lies in its ledger, never to be shared again.

You rap on the door with curled fingers and wait as a breeze blows leaves across the stone steps. Silence fills the front driveway, and you knock again, but there's no answer and you're filled with relief at not having to face the demons right now.

You try the doorbell, and a faint familiar chime rings out from inside the home. It's the same sound you remember from Thanksgivings-past when carloads of guests would arrive with spouses and children and smiles and dishes to share. It's the sound you'd heard thousands of times on nights and weekends when dinner party guests arrived with wine, presents, and flowers. It's a reminder of Halloween trick-or-treaters arriving on the stoop in Batman and Catwoman masks, ready to fill their pillowcases. You look down at your finger and find the doorbell is the same cracked yellow plastic button from the time you lived here.

A lock is being turned and the door opens to reveal a pair of watery blue eyes on a woman short in stature. There's a volume of dyed blonde hair on her head, and she wears a white T-shirt and black slacks. She can't be more than five feet tall, with sunken cheeks and wrinkled skin pale like ash. Her eyes, once bright blue, are rheumy and distant, but sparkle briefly upon seeing your face.

"Clay. My god. What happened to your face...and your hair?"

"It was an accident, Mom. I'm OK."

"Come here, son," she says, reaching out for hug, but you take a step back, brushing her off.

"Not right now."

"My god, son. How are you?"

"Not good, Mom. I was wondering if you could maybe...Could you hold me one last time?" Your throat is tight and you feel the emotion on your face.

"I just tried to hug you but you pushed me away...Please come in, son. I've missed you. What's it been? Twenty years?"

"Why did you lie?"

"I don't know what you're talking about."

"That only makes it worse."

"Oh, son. Let's forget the past. It's time to move on."

"I don't want to live there either, but I can't make sense of the present without knowing the truth."

She runs a hand through her thick yellow pompadour.

"You may not believe it, son, but I did...*we* did the best we could." Her face is scrunched up and her lips are quivering.

"*You did the best you could?* That's rich. There's still pencil lead in my hand where you stabbed me that would disagree with your parenting assessment."

"Oh, Clay."

"I hurt all the time, Mom. I'm constantly scared. Could you hold me and tell me the truth?"

"Everything's OK now, baby."

"But it's *not* OK! What happened to Paul!?"

"Cancer, Clay. Basal cell carcinoma. I'm sorry he's gone, baby."

"Where's Dad buried?"

"Same place as Paul. The plot at Golf Creek. He was cremated...But how are *you*, son? I heard you found love."

"I found it, but I don't know what to do with it, Mom. I'm scared all the time, and I don't trust anyone. I'm afraid I'll get hurt again."

She's hanging on the door and gripping its edges, leaning on the handle for support while still looking at you with those watery blue eyes.

"I pushed away love because I was afraid. I've said *I love you* thousands of times but never once meant it. I never felt the emotion behind my words, and not because I was cruel, but because I couldn't trust anyone. I saw love in the movies and on TV, but never related to the clichés of 'butterflies' or 'fireworks' at seeing someone I cared about. Imagine–"

"Clay, I–"

"I never knew safety, Mom, so I spent my life frightened of people and things. Rampant and irrational fears that led to panic attacks and crying. I isolated and hurt myself because that's all I knew. I have constant flashbacks of violence and trauma—like a war veteran—and all I am is lonely."

"Why do we have to talk about this, son? Let's move on."

"I can't shake the memories of the past. I remember being held down in the bathtub and–"

"I'm so tired, Clay. I have diabetes and–" she says.

"I remember the yellow telephone in the kitchen, Mom. I remember the curled yellow cord wrapped tightly around–"

"I really need to lie down, Clay. My heart condition, you know."

"What were you thinking?"

A sports car zooms by on the street, and we both turn and look as it disappears down the block with a squeal of brakes. There's the sound of leaves bristling in the trees from the wind.

"You were a very difficult child. So loud and with so much energy. Always talking and running around. I didn't know...I had no time for myself because you took everything from me. I slept two hours a night for years."

"I was a baby. That's what babies do."

"I'm tired. It's time for my medication, Clay. I need to lie down."

"How come you can't face the truth? I was a beautiful boy with everything going for me. I had it all and you ruined everything! Everything!"

"You'll always be my little boy. Come here."

"I'm already dead, Mom. It only looks like I'm alive."

"I failed you and I know it." She's crying now and holding the door handle. "Why did you come here, son?"

"To see you before I die. I want to die before you, Mom, because it's the only way I can hurt you, pay you back for what you did."

"There's nothing I can say that will satisfy you." Her hand rises to her face and wipes her eyes.

"That's not true. I want the truth."

She shuffles in the doorway and sighs. "How could that possibly help?"

"Because you can't build a relationship on lies."

"I'm glad you want a relationship with me, son."

"I didn't say I did."

"You've been through so much. Let me hold you, Clay. You're my darling little boy."

"Why do you want to hold me? Is it for you or for me?"

"No more lies, Clay, I promise."

"When did you start to—"

"From the day you were born."

"I want to know every—"

"Your father...all he did was work. I sat alone with you and your brother every day, and I was overwhelmed. A young mother with two infants and no experience. I had sewing needles that I'd poke on your skin to keep you boys awake so you'd sleep through the night. Just little pin pricks throughout the day when you got tired. But you'd scream when I hurt you. Boy would you scream. So I'd..." She's sobbing now.

"Keep going! Tell me everything!"

"I wanted to see how much you could take, but you were tough. Then there was the bathtub and I...I don't want to talk about it, son. You were terrified of swimming lessons, and I always knew why."

"And Dad?"

"Your father liked you and your brother, and I tried to keep...It was either you or—"

"Tell me about the cough medicine you made us drink every day." She stares at you silently. "How do you think you did as a human being, Mom? How will you be remembered?"

"I don't think any more, son...My bones are weak and frail...It's over for me, but you still have a chance to build something."

"*Are you out of your fucking mind!?* My foundation is cracked, my wood is warped, my walls have dry rot, my nails are bent, there's no roof, and it's constantly raining. How am I going to build a future like this?"

"I'm sorry, Clay. You have to try."

And now your legs are hurting, and you feel the need to sit, so you slump on the stoop as the mailman arrives. He sees the two of you crying and says nothing, just drops off the mail off with a cheery smile, then descends the front steps.

"Please come in, son. Everything I have is yours."

"That's rich."

"You're so angry."

"No shit."

"You can heal. I promise. It's possible."

"It's *not* possible, Mom. It's been four decades and I'm still broken!"

"Why won't you come in, son?"

"Because..."

"Come in. You've built such a wonderful career, and I'm so proud of you! Why won't you come in and sit with me in our home?"

"Because..."

"Please."

"No, Mom."

"Why not?"

"Because it's...*it's what you want.*" You're on the ground with tears running down your face and your shoulders shaking, the concrete cold against your skin.

"I love you, son."

"Bullshit. You never showed it. You never protected me. I never received an ounce of kindness, except for the last cheeseburger you gave me at dinnertime."

"I wasn't perfect, but I loved you. Please come in. What you have is a home."

"What I have are nightmares, flashbacks, and a dozen prescriptions."

"I really need to take my medicine. Come in."

"I promised I never would. Goodbye, Mom." You turn and walk down the stone steps to your car and hear footsteps behind you. You turn to see her carefully limping down the steps behind you.

"Please don't go! You're all I have left! I know I failed you, but I'm still a human being!"

You turn back to look at her from the driveway with the car keys jangling in your hand.

"What kind of human being does this to a child?" There's silence from her as she looks at you. "Imagine a parent who could do this to another human being."

"I was a child, too, and I have some personal experience in this area."

"So!? My heart is supposed to bleed for you? At least you survived! You made it! You've had a ton of friends, a job, multiple homes, vacations anytime you want, and bulging bank accounts."

"Come back. I'll finally hold you like you want to be held. I promise I'll never let you go. I'll hold you close for as long as you want, and I promise you can have as much love as you need until I take my final breath."

"You killed me. You destroyed the very thing you created." You open the door to the car and turn back to look at her with a face covered in tears.

"You're my beautiful boy. I'm sorry, son. I'm so sorry. I'd do anything to fix this." And now she's crouched on a step like a seedling in an elementary school play, shaking and sobbing. The wind blows leaves across the driveway, and there's the sound of traffic in the distance.

"Goodbye, Mom. Take care."

There's sobbing as you fumble with the keys, open the door, and sit in the driver's seat. The door closes with a thunk, and you settle in on an otherwise perfect day. You start the engine and look at her sitting and sobbing, then put the car into drive and turn out onto the street.

20

INDIA IS BASICALLY A PARTICLE accelerator where dozens of cultures are excited into a frenzy and smashed together at atomic speed. Forget the diversity of Papua New Guinea or Tanzania, because they've got nothing on the action happening here. Hinduism, Islam, Christianity, Sikhism, Buddhism, Jainism, Zoroastrianism, Judaism, and other religions coexist in a nation of over a billion people. You can't find this much cultural intermingling anywhere else in the world.

The stereotypes would have you reduce India to its most cringe-worthy elements. It's a nation of poverty and diarrhea, where Mumbai call center employees dupe their callers into believing they're stateside workers. (*"Hello, this is Andrew. How may I be of assistance to you today?"*) Indian men are either satyrs or eunuchs according to the stereotypes, either horn dogs with raging boners from the Kama Sutra or asexual naïfs. The West still thinks turbans and pajamas are the style here.

In my mind, the Indian myths have less to do with malice than with a deficit of cultural information. The West and India are myopic in their worldviews and could use a kick in the pants to look beyond their borders.

Western news websites get the blame in my book because of their focus on click bait. Camera phone footage of ethnic violence, tourist attacks, snake charmers, bride burnings, and child labor appeal to our prurient interests and generate big bucks online. News websites make money from page views, after all, so they'll do anything to entice a click or tap from digital passersby.

The result is a Western news focus that's fashioned India into a freakish horror show with headlines to match. There's no money to be made from featuring India as an economic powerhouse or cultural nexus, because who cares about that? INDIA GDP DOUBLES SINCE 2014 or TOURIST BITTEN BY BAG OF SNAKES ON MUMBAI TRAIN. Which link do you think more people click? Click bait is the only way websites make money.

These news websites don't care about your experience after you've taken the "bait," because the sites have already been paid by their overlords. Advertisers pay websites as soon as visitors arrive, so these sites have as much interest in you after you get there as a dog has in its owner after doggie dinnertime. In fact, all these news sites have to do is lure you with the *promise* of something salacious and their coffers grow.

In my mind, you'll never have balanced news coverage of India until profits are removed from the news business. Every news organization will tell you the same thing: Conventional news has a zero profit margin.

These online schlock and awe campaigns have been in effect since the dawn of the web, but I've maintained my positive regard for India because of my career. Pilots don't make decisions without collecting data from multiple sources. In fact, independent verification is a hallmark of aviation, because our profession is obsessed with safety.

All of this is my long way of saying the seamy stories about India never dissuaded me in my travels because I was open to learning the truth when I got here. Sure, the online stories angered and annoyed me, but they never dampened my enthusiasm for the Jewel in the Crown.

• • •

I returned to Kolkata and the people at the Home welcomed me back with many warm smiles and hugs. The volunteers even threw me a little party upstairs with some cake and tea as Sister Anancia held my hand in front of a few dozen people. She made a little speech as I stood there half-smiling but mostly looking at my feet and trying to figure out what it meant. There was the occasion's warmth and the joy at being back, but I couldn't shake my grief over Plim and the sorrow of being away from home.

The volunteers opened their hearts to me, and their small tribute meant the world because it touched my soul. I guess they knew what had happened and why I was there, but didn't know what to say. Maybe the party was their way of reaching out and telling me they cared. If it was, it worked.

Later, I stood alone on the balcony and looked out onto the sun-drenched courtyard where kids played soccer and workers tended the garden. I helped myself to another piece of cake and marveled at the calm as shadows grew like geometric shapes on the ground. My watch reminded me I was due downstairs to start my shift soon, so I put my things in my locker and got changed.

Sumito Goldberg was captured by the FBI shortly after the Times Square hotel debacle. He, in turn, gave up Matt's involvement in the whole affair. The two had been in cahoots to promote Swoosh Airlines, and lots of money exchanged hands. I was merely a pawn in the whole scheme, useful to Matt and Sumito for awhile until I grew suspicious and surmised who was behind it all. Even now, I wish I could have thirty minutes alone with Matt to find out what he was thinking. I have a ton of questions but I doubt the answers would really give me any relief.

Saying I miss Plim isn't the half of it. I feel like I'm one of the walking wounded, parading around as a shell of myself with an injury that won't heal. *I wish I could see her one more time.* That's what I tell myself at all hours when I'm feeling down and needing the comfort of her touch. I wonder what she'd say if she could see me now, and then I smile thinking of her, because she'd probably use her air quotes and say something snarky to make me smile.

There's something going in East India that's bigger than culture or volunteering or novelty—and it's something no travel books or essays can convey. There's a generosity here you can only find in the wind and the shade, and it will change you.

And it's this very beauty that makes checking my emails and texts from the States so disquieting. Sam Varsick texts me with links to articles that blight Kolkata in the region's tired clichés. *Watch out for jaundice, leptospirosis, cholera, and tuberculosis, bro! Get on your fucking camel and get yourself to a pharmacy, OK?!*

It's enervating to argue and dismantle the stereotypes, so I've taken a different tack and found solace in talking with the tourists who come here. The tourists arrive with action-packed agendas and hopes of attending the festivals they've heard so much about. So, I do my part and bolster their feelings of warmth with my own brand of goodwill.

Tourists flock to Diwali and Holi and are quick to claim spiritual enlightenment. I smile at their stories and would never deconstruct their joy. The Hindu Festival of Lights and Festival of Colors are beautiful, but they're only a fraction of the warmth in the nation's heart. What I really want to tell the tourists is to stay here, because that's the only way their love can blossom.

The tourist set arrive and act much as I did when I first came, both fascinated and frightened by the cultural shock. They work hard to mask their feelings behind sunglasses and forced smiles, and I can't say I blame them. It takes time getting used to East India and I don't judge them for being ill at ease.

In fact, I encourage tourists to do every touristy thing they want when they arrive, and would never deign to lecture them about the "real" India. People should fashion a trip to their own tastes, not mine, because it's their vacation. And there's no shame in snapping a selfie in front of the Taj Mahal or doing the "holding the spire like a spinning top" photo cliché, because every tourist does the same. Go ahead. No judgment here.

Even the stares used to bother me because they called attention to my differences, but now I embrace my personality as my own superpower. Having a different style of dress, manner, and culture is a strength that helps me start conversations and build deep bonds.

But being here has me divided because I'm both happy and sullen. Happy with the people and my work, but grief-stricken over the past and my attempts to move forward. I want a break from the hurt in my heart, to be able to enjoy new friendships, and I can't do that without letting go. I'm still trying to make sense of the year before.

The chief issue here has been Randala, Plim's wife, who moved here after Plim's death. I can't figure out why I'm so uptight around her, but I'm in knots even though we have so much in common. I tiptoed around her at the party earlier even as we exchanged short words about our sorrow. Today, though, I need to shadow Randala for my training, and it's got my stomach churning.

• • •

I arrive on the men's ward in my apron, shorts, bandana, and flip-flops to find Randala moving between cots on the ward's south side.

"Hi, Clay. Why don't you get started with the items on the clipboard, OK?" she says.

"Sure. All right."

"Do you need anything in particular?" she says.

"No, I'm good. Ready to go."

"Check the log book on the wall and start anywhere you want. You can run the water for the baths. That's a good place to start."

"OK."

That interchange is what suffices for "management" here, and although it's a far cry from the cockpit, it's actually all I need to keep me going. I don't mind being second in command, a dutiful first officer, and so I do everything I'm asked because I'm accustomed to hierarchy. And yet neither of us is making much eye contact despite working nearly side by side.

"How's the bath water? OK?"

"It's fine. All good."

"We could take a break," Randala says.

"No, I'm good."

These short back-and-forth interchanges are becoming our norm and they drive me crazy with their superficiality. I want to get real. Randala and I shouldn't be coworkers— we should be the closest of friends, bound by our common grief. We should be closer than close, I think, but I'm lonely and needy and too stuck in my head to know what's what. *I wonder what she's going through. What can I do for her?* There's a hand on my shoulder and I startle.

"Do you miss...her?" Randala says.

I sigh. "She used to...I'm sorry. I don't know what to say to you."

"There's nothing you can say...Why weren't you at her memorial service?" Randala says.

"I don't know. I don't have a good answer for that."

"Plim said you were always hurting."

"She told you that?!" I laugh. "I'm ashamed to admit it."

"What's wrong with being yourself?" she says.

"Nobody wants to be around someone lonely and needy!" I laugh some more.

"Do you want me to hold you?" Randala says.

"No! No. I'm over that!" I say and my face begins to quiver. "It's OK. Thank you."

"Plim said that was the only thing that made you happy,"

"It was...but...Now there's something else. You don't have to do anything for me. What can I do for you?"

She considers me for a few seconds without talking.

"Walk over here for a minute," she says, standing up. I follow her to a prep area behind a privacy curtain where two volunteers are talking. She takes off her apron and gloves, and I do the same.

My arms warp around her in a hug and she sobs on my shoulder in great heaves like waves crashing ashore. I hold her close with my hands rubbing her back, and try to stay strong. Her shoulders hunch, and I push down my own sadness so I can be the rock for her. She grips me tighter and my face presses into her shirt, soaking it with my tears.

"I'm sorry. So, so sorry. I–" I say.

"I'm learning how to be OK with it not being OK. Maybe that's the key." She wipes her eyes and looks at me thoughtfully.

"I guess so," I say.

Maybe it's no one's fault I'm broken. What happened in the past *happened,* and it's unrealistic to expect India or Randala or anyone else to fix that. Everyone here's been accommodating and I've slipped right back into the routine—except I still feel disconnected.

For starters, I need to up my language game and become fluent in the local dialects. I have to throw myself into the volunteer activities, including soccer in the courtyard, evening drinks, Scrabble, and chess—always chess—so I'll be viewed as team member.

Still, I have to reconcile the fact I'm not one of the shiny gap-year kids who arrive here between studies and soon return home. These twenty- and thirtysomethings arrive fresh-faced and full of hope like freshmen on the first day of college. They're the Home's backbone, and I do enjoy seeing their bright smiles and thick mops of hair because they're on their way to bright futures and bulging bank accounts. I only wish I'd had half their poise when I was their age.

I want to protect the rose-colored worlds of these young people filled with promise and wonder. They don't deserve to be weighed down. The Germans, French, and Kenyans

I've met will soon return home to friends and families, schools and marriages. They'll build their careers, have families, and remember Kolkata as a series of social media memories. But what of me and my journey? How should I document my time here, and should I ever return home, wherever that may be?

Returning to Manhattan's Midtown seems laughable at this point, now that I'm old and out of touch. I'm past my prime and can't easily integrate into the city as upstart, hipster, artist, or heathen. I can't start over because I missed that bus a long time ago.

Other times, I realize how fortunate I am to have had this life, and I can't imagine being anywhere else. Sure, I'd kill for some temaki sushi or a greasy burrito, but I can't even get my hands on a PB&J here without a serious sojourn to a Western supermarket. But the food, language, and the culture here aren't the half of it, because the heat and transportation are daily struggles. And if you could see where I live now! I'm in a dorm—never thought I'd do that again.

"How are you? You OK?" Randala says with a hand on my shoulder.

"Am I doing something wrong?" I'm back in my gloves and apron, giving a patient a sponge bath.

"No, no. You're doing fine. Let me know if you need anything."

It's hard to reconcile the years of "friendship" I thought I had with Matt with the reality that came into being. I miss the café talks with Plim on 9th Ave and the connection we shared. It's hard to think of these memories in place ten thousand miles away. Where do I belong now?

I miss flying and the intellectual challenge of the cockpit, but that part of my life vanished when I separated from

RASH. The party girls and nightlife I don't miss at all—they were the easiest to bid farewell. Maybe I can reinvent myself and adopt Randala's philosophy: *Just be OK with it not being OK.*

"Clay, sorry! Can you give me a hand over here?" Randala says from across the ward.

"Sure." I head over, straightening my apron, then itch my nose with the crook of my elbow, keeping my gloved hands away from my face.

"We need to put some moisturizer on him for his bed sores. Do you mind giving me a hand?" she says.

"I can do it. Go ahead and do whatever you need to do. I've got it," I say looking at her. "I...I just can't stop thinking about her."

"Me too. Plim was warm to everyone," Randala says softly.

I scoop some moisturizer into my gloves and rub my hands together, spreading it on my palms.

"I guess this is my journey," she says.

"That's what I always say!" I laugh.

"By the way, Clay, this is Tamik," she says, touching the man's arm next to us.

I look at Tamik's gray face and notice the crags that line it and the red in the whites of his eyes. He's probably in his thirties, but his face is too wrinkled and ashen for such a young man. I wonder what's wrong with him. Randala reaches for the moisturizing compound and puts a big dollop in her gloved hand without noticing I've done the same thing.

"Randala, seriously. I've got it. Let me do it." She nods and sighs and rubs the ball of compound onto my hands, then stands and heads toward the break room.

"I'm going to sit you up, OK? It's going to hurt a little, but we need to rotate you." I pull Tamik into a sitting position and wrap my arms around him in a hug. He groans as I rub my hands into his shoulders and back, then ease him back down. I roll him onto his side, rest a gloved hand on his arm, and watch his chest rise and fall. He sighs.

I take his hand in both of mine and stroke it gently as he breathes softly. His hand is wrapped in a sandwich of yellow latex, and I notice the contrast of the clinical and the human so close together. I reach down and pull off my right-hand glove, then the other, and I sigh.

I caress Tamik's hand in mine, and I feel mutual warmth exchanged, a volume of heat pouring into my flesh from his. I take another scoop of moisturizer in my fingers and rub it on his shoulders and arms, then turn him onto his stomach and caress his back, and notice his eyes watering.

"Here you go, man. We're good. It's better now."

I roll him onto his back and rest my bare hand on his chest, then rub the moisturizer on his arms and hands, skin on skin. I'm sitting there next to his cot and I hear voices on the ward's south side. I can't hear what they're saying. I continue touching him and the most satisfying sigh escapes my soul.

I look at him, and for a moment, I swear I see a smile on his face as his eyes catch the light. And there's a smile on mine, too.

About Brian Barton

I always wanted to write, and I used to create stories when I was a teenager to entertain my friends. Every book starts with research, so I like to read, travel, and interview people, taking notes on what I learn. I'll immerse myself in a subject because it's interesting, and then I'll start writing. Completing a book takes years, but the journey's worth it. When I'm done, I'll work with an editor on the manuscript and with an artist to create the book's design. My goal is to refine the story's essence so I can immerse you in its world. I'm an independent author, and I'm grateful for your support.

Acknowledgments

Thanks to the pilots, security, and law enforcement professionals who sat down with me for interviews as far back as 2012. This work wouldn't exist without you. Please forgive any inaccuracies or exaggerations herein done in the name of storytelling.

Thanks to my family, friends, and the professional cadre who float me on every creative trip. Thanks especially to: Bill, D.M.T, Dave, Emily, Gymrats, J.Y, Joe, Julia, Linda, NYC Wordwrap, Phil, Red to Black Editing, Robert, and Write Klear Software.

—B.B.

New York City